EAT WHAT YOU KILL

EAT WHAT YOU KILL

Becoming a Sales Carnivore

Sam Taggart

PORTFOLIO · PENGUIN

PORTFOLIO / PENGUIN
An imprint of Penguin Random House LLC
penguinrandomhouse.com

Most Portfolio books are available at a discount when purchased in
quantity for sales promotions or corporate use. Special editions, which
include personalized covers, excerpts, and corporate imprints, can be created
when purchased in large quantities. For more information, please call
(212) 572-2232 or email specialmarkets@penguinrandomhouse.com.
Your local bookstore can also assist with discounted bulk purchases using the
Penguin Random House corporate Business-to-Business program. For assistance
in locating a participating retailer, email B2B@penguinrandomhouse.com.

LIBRARY OF CONGRESS CATALOGING-IN-PUBLICATION DATA
Names: Taggart, Sam (Founder of D2D Experts), author.
Title: Eat what you kill: becoming a sales carnivore / Sam Taggart.
Description: [New York] : Portfolio/Penguin, [2025]
Identifiers: LCCN 2024031209 (print) | LCCN 2024031210 (ebook) |
ISBN 9780593715741 (hardcover) | ISBN 9780593715772 (ebook)
Subjects: LCSH: Selling. | Success in business. | Deals.
Classification: LCC HF5438.25 .T34 2025 (print) | LCC HF5438.25 (ebook) |
DDC 658.85—dc23/eng/20240806
LC record available at https://lccn.loc.gov/2024031209
LC ebook record available at https://lccn.loc.gov/2024031210

Printed in the United States of America
1st Printing

BOOK DESIGN BY TANYA MAIBORODA

To my dad, Paul—my first sales teacher and entrepreneurial mentor, who inspired me to chase my dreams.

Contents

PART THREE

Nonverbal Selling

PART FOUR

Prospecting

PART FIVE

Pitching

PART SIX

Presenting

PART SEVEN

Objections

Introduction: Eat What You Kill

THE BEST WAY TO classify different kinds of salespeople isn't dividing them up by *what* they sell, such as cars or real estate or life insurance or B2B cloud storage.

It also isn't dividing them up by *how* they sell, such as by making appointments with retailers, cold-calling, standing on the floor of a store, or knocking on the doors of strangers.

Instead, the crucial divide—the one that makes all the difference— is between herbivores and carnivores. That's the core idea of this book.

You may recall your third-grade teacher explaining that herbivore dinosaurs are the kind that eat plants. If you got dropped into Jurassic Park, you could walk right up to an herbivore and pat him on the side without fear of being eaten, because he would just keep munching grass and leaves.

Similarly, herbivore salespeople live on whatever sustenance— leads—happen to be right in front of them, or within easy reach. Herbivores rely on someone else, usually their employer, to give them quality leads or set up appointments for them. Imagine a car salesman sitting around a dealership, doing nothing until a prospect walks in, drawn by an ad or email blast. That guy is an herbivore.

As long as an external source provides enough good leads, herbivores can thrive and might even make good money. The downside is that they can only be as successful as the quality of their next lead. When good leads dry up, they are in serious trouble. They'll start worrying constantly about where their next prospect is coming from. And if times get tough for the company, herbivores are the first to be let go.

Carnivore dinosaurs, on the other hand, eat animals, including other dinosaurs. They have the mindset of a born hunter, and they eat what they kill. They are the equivalent of salespeople who don't need anyone to hand them a list of prospects or schedule their appointments. Instead, carnivores create unlimited opportunities by cold-calling, knocking doors, tapping into their own networks, using Google or public databases, and any other means they can think of. Carnivores don't depend on their employers to be successful. By eating what they kill, and constantly honing their hunting skills, they never have to worry about starving. But they have to be willing to work harder and longer and endure more rejection than herbivores.

There's also a third type of dinosaur, the omnivore, who can switch back and forth between plants and meat. Sales omnivores can do their own prospecting and referral generation, or they can work with leads provided by their employer's marketing funnel. This flexibility is valuable, but omnivores derive their greatest value from their carnivore skills and mindset.

Across all my experience as a salesperson, sales manager, sales coach, and trainer of sales coaches, I've seen that herbivores vastly outnumber carnivores and omnivores. This imbalance is bad news for herbivores, because there are limited opportunities for anyone who needs to have leads spoon-fed to them. But it's *excellent* news for carnivores, who will always be in high demand. Smart companies make sure their carnivores are well compensated and well treated or they won't stick around long.

If you get really good at eating what you kill, you'll enjoy a massive competitive advantage and a clear path to wealth, job security, and a high quality of life for yourself and your family. That's why my goal is to teach you everything you need to know to be a true carnivore, from mindset and big-picture strategies to nitty-gritty tactics that have been proven to really work.

I've found that some sales reps start out as carnivores in their early years, but somewhere along the way they lose their hunting mentality. They take a job where someone else sets up their leads, and they get complacent and a little lazy. It's just human nature to let someone else hand you plants instead of spending all day chasing down gazelles. Once you start down that path, it's hard to recover the discipline and focus of a carnivore. Hard, but not impossible! If you're in this category, keep reading and commit to turning things around.

The highest-earning salespeople I've ever met don't give in to the temptation to take easier jobs. They stay hungry, sharp, and self-reliant well into their thirties, forties, fifties, and beyond. They keep chasing those gazelles. As a result, they're protected when marketing pipelines dry up, or algorithms that formerly brought in prospects stop working. Yesterday's hot new lead-generation tactic, such as Facebook ads, can easily become today's dead end. But a carnivore can roll with changing times and changing technology, and keep making money.

As you'll see throughout this book, the majority of sales success depends on your mindset and managing your emotions. Strategies and tactics are also important, of course, but they always come second. And the mindset stuff isn't easy to master. For instance, carnivores need to stay calm and keep moving forward, whether they're having the best or worst sales day of their lives. They need to maintain emotional stability, rather than getting super excited when on a hot streak and super depressed when they repeatedly fail. You can learn how to find that kind of calm focus.

Please note—this is really important—words like *carnivore* and *kill* don't mean you should aim to hurt, exploit, or metaphorically kill your customers. Just the opposite! You want them to feel good when a transaction is over. You want them to be grateful because you solved some kind of problem for them. You want them to love you so much that they'll recommend you to their friends.

You want to be killing your goals, killing your competitors, killing any flawed thinking that's holding you back—but *never* killing your customers.

It has always bothered me that salespeople get such a bad rap, like we're all sleazy, self-serving, and manipulative. I think there's a very clear line between using psychology and empathy to win a sale and manipulating people into a sale. I always try to stay on the right side of that line, and I'll teach you to do likewise.

Part of my mission in life is to bring more dignity to the reputation of the entire sales industry. We should be seen as an honorable profession, because sales is the lubricant of society. Everything people use had to be sold in one way or another, including the food you eat and the bed you sleep on. So I will never accept that sales is bad or shameful or dishonorable. Done right, sales is about creating positive experiences and win-win scenarios, through a skillful use of perception, framing, communication, and empathy. I've found it endlessly fascinating since I was a kid. Still do.

Speaking of when I was a kid, before we go any further, I should tell you a little about myself. Otherwise, like any prospect, you might be wondering why you should believe anything I have to say. Here's why. . . .

How I Got Here

MY NEXT BIRTHDAY CAKE will still have fewer than thirty-five candles, but I've done and seen a lot in the world of sales. In fact, I've been studying and practicing sales since childhood, constantly experimenting to figure out what works, what doesn't, and why.

Some people discover the excitement of selling as adults, others as teenagers. For me, the sales bug goes all the way back to my childhood in Utah. It started with some door-to-door candy sale fundraisers, around age seven. Then during the summer when I was eight, I started my first business, selling used golf balls.

I can't remember who suggested it, but my plan was simple. Every evening that summer, I'd walk around the local course after the golfers were done. I'd fish Titleists out of ponds, scan the rough for TaylorMades, and search the nearby woods for shots that had gone way off course. Then on Saturday I'd bring my buckets of balls to a folding table on the back nine, where golfers happily paid me to refill their ammo. I soon realized I could sell them more than balls, so I asked my mom to buy bags of chips in bulk at Costco, plus some giant bottles of lemonade and plastic cups. Some Saturdays I went home with a hundred bucks, which was serious money! I was thrilled—until the owners of the golf course caught wind and banned me from the property.

When I was eleven, my brother got me to help him sell coupon books door to door to promote local businesses, including bowling alleys and restaurants, and tickets to the Utah Jazz. He was ten years older than me, and I thought he had the whole world figured out. Each time I sold a coupon book, we split the twenty-dollar commission. I realized that making ten dollars for a sale was good, but making ten dollars from someone else's work was even better. I filed that away for future reference.

When I turned thirteen, my cousin introduced me to an even better sales idea: painting house numbers on curbs. He taught me how to knock on a stranger's door and ask if visitors ever had trouble seeing their address from the street. If so, I explained, they might have a big problem if they needed the police or fire department in an emergency. I could solve their problem and make the house easy to identify, for just twenty dollars.

If my two-minute pitch worked (which it usually did), I'd use a stencil and spray-paint the curb, and ten minutes later I'd be off to the next house. If my pitch didn't work, or if someone was rude or even slammed the door on me, I learned to shrug it off. And if I closed five sales an hour, that was one hundred dollars—more than ten times what other middle school kids might make by babysitting or scooping ice cream. I got addicted to the "seller's high" of closing, and spoiled from all the cash at my disposal, even after paying for expenses.

A year later, when my family moved to California, I became the new kid at a new high school. I figured I could make some new friends and scale my business at the same time. I convinced eleven other guys to sell curb numbers the same way I did, and gave them everything they needed, including supplies, a sales script, and a schedule of which streets to hit on which afternoons. In return, they agreed to pay me eight dollars for every twenty dollars they collected from a homeowner.

In other words, at age fourteen I wasn't just a salesman, I was a *sales manager*. I tried to make our operation professional, ordering T-shirts that read "The Gutterman." We even had a MySpace page, which was cutting-edge marketing at the time.

I had to get really organized, because we kept running out of paint, stencils, tape, and scrapers. Did you know that if a high school kid tries to buy enough spray paint to cover every wall in town, the store is supposed to call the cops? I had to ask my mom to go around to various stores to pick up our spray paint, like a bootlegger during Prohibition.

Not long ago my dad found my old computer files from that business, including my ledger of sales, the schedule of names and streets, and the script I wrote for my reps. It was a pretty good script for a kid with no sales training. It included stage directions like "Slow down here. . . . Pause after this line. . . . Now change your inflection to get excited." It all came from trial and error. If something worked for me, I added it to the script.

Right after my high school graduation, my brother hit me up because one of his friends owned an alarm systems company called Platinum Protection. I figured with all my experience in curb painting, I could rock a summer job doing grown-up door-to-door sales. So on a Friday in mid-June I shipped off to Dallas—my first extended time away from home. Didn't know a soul in town. The local manager, a guy named Luke, was supposed to pick me up at the airport, but he was four hours late because he was too busy closing sales.

Before I even went to drop my luggage at the apartment where I'd be staying, I shadowed Luke for the last couple of hours of his day, watching him close two sales. Then he dropped me off at my apartment, leaving me with a training packet, three blank contracts, a company shirt, and an assigned neighborhood for the next day. At this point I didn't even know how an alarm system worked, but the next morning I was going to be a professional D2D rep.

You'll find out what happened the next day later in the book, along with some other fun stories about my early years in D2D sales. For now, just to fast-forward, I can tell you I got better and better through a mix of coaching, self-education, and trial and error. Before long I was making enough money that it didn't seem worth it to go back to college at Utah Valley University. For nearly a decade (2008 to 2017), I was a top-rated sales rep and worked my way up to sales manager. Then I became a VP of sales in two industries, alarms and solar.

But by 2017, I felt a strong urge to do something bigger than just continuing to boost my sales income. I wanted to share my success as widely as possible, while also unifying, upleveling, and bringing more honor and integrity to the sales profession—especially the widely disrespected practice of D2D. So I quit my $600,000 a year job and started my own training, consulting, and events company, the D2D Experts. We hosted our first annual convention, D2DCon, in January 2018. Positive buzz about us spread, and we've been growing ever since.

These days I feel blessed to have an eight-figure, kick-ass company and a much wider audience, helping tens of thousands of salespeople achieve the success of their dreams. My team now draws more than four thousand attendees to each D2DCon and thousands more to about fifteen other events each year. We have about ten thousand active monthly users on our online platform for D2D professionals. More than forty thousand users have participated in our online video training courses.

Building the D2D Experts has been an incredible learning experience. I had to figure out how to sell conference tickets, elite mastermind groups, and six-figure consulting packages for businesses. We even started three successful software platforms for salespeople: Recruit-o-Matic, Vanilla Message, and Xpand. Our newest software project, Xpand, is a human development coaching platform that will help individuals and companies enjoy personal growth and better quality of life.*

All these new products and services forced me to sharpen my B2B sales and sales management skills, in completely different directions than I had ever attempted before. Sometimes it feels like a very long way from golf balls and curb painting.

But in another sense, it isn't very different at all. Ultimately, sales is sales is sales. It's a set of skills, strategies, and mindsets that anyone can learn, practice, master, and adapt to new settings.

And now, with this book, I'm excited to share this essential knowledge even more widely. So let's get into it.

---

* You can learn more about our software products, conferences, and other offerings at the back of the book, or at thed2dexperts.com.

PART ONE

Mindset

1

Introduction to Mindset

YOU MIGHT BE CHAMPING at the bit to dive into the details of what to say to prospects so you can close more sales. We're going to cover all of that, but first we have to address the super-important subject of mindset.

If the word *mindset* sounds too woo-woo for you, just think of it as the unspoken thoughts rattling around inside your head. I *know* you have those, because we all do. Whether you realize it or not, you have stories that you silently tell yourself about your strengths and weaknesses, your past performance, your future goals and expectations, your prospects and customers, and what defines success, mediocrity, and failure. Those statements and stories are always there, whether you notice them or not.

This really matters because, as Brian Tracy put it, "Sales success is 80 percent attitude and only 20 percent aptitude." Your subconscious attitude might be telling you that you're the best salesperson in the world, or a total loser, or somewhere in between—and you will act accordingly. Once you accept that 80 percent of your results flow from unspoken or even unnoticed beliefs, you'd better get really freaking good at shaping those beliefs.

In this section we will go beyond the usual rah-rah motivational sayings, to help you adopt the full mindset of a high-performing sales carnivore. You'll get a lot more clarity about your goals, your perceptions of what you can (and can't) accomplish, and your attitudes about competition, rejection, and much more.

Success has to start in your head before it can be manifested in reality. So let's change the stories you tell yourself, which will change your state of mind, which will then change your results. I've seen this happen in my own life and career, a story I told in depth in my previous book, *The Self Xperience*.

My view of success has been shaped by four simple but universal laws that smart people have been noticing for centuries.

The first is the *law of attraction*, also known as manifestation, which some dismiss as a superstition. But it's really human psychology, not anything supernatural. If you want to see real progress in your results, you have to set explicit goals and remind yourself of those goals every day. Become obsessed with your goals, whether that's hitting a certain income level, improving your closing ratio, or something else. Visualize in your mind's eye what your life will look like once you get there.

One effective tactic is to let yourself feel like you've already achieved those goals, by writing affirmations in the present or past tense, not the future (for example, "I made $100,000" rather than "I will make $100,000"). If you repeat such affirmations daily, you will subconsciously begin to do the action steps that will drive the success you seek. As the saying goes, sometimes you have to see it to believe it, but sometimes you have to believe it before you can see it.

The second law is the *law of gravity*. When Isaac Newton saw an apple fall from a tree in 1666, he realized that an invisible force is pulling everything downward. Gravity is neither good nor bad; it's just reality. When that apple hit the ground, that was where it was supposed to be at that moment. You, too, are wherever you're supposed to be at this point in your journey—so there's no need to be discouraged by your current status.

I look at this from a religious perspective, but even if you don't believe that God shapes our paths, the law of gravity still applies. We're all on a unique journey that may not make sense until we get near the end. Some of us have a rockier path, and some have a smoother path, but we're all doing our best against the gravity pulling us downward. Therefore we're all worthy of respect, no matter where we currently stand. Never trash-talk yourself by thinking something like *I'm not worthy yet, but I will be after I hit my goals.* That's not true! The mere act of living and pushing back against gravity makes you worthy.

The third law is one I made up, the *law of GOYA*. That's an acronym for GET OFF YOUR ASS. So many people think they can just think or meditate their way to success. But all of your thinking, including all the mindset tactics in this section of the book, needs to lead to action. Thinking without action won't help you.

When you embrace the law of attraction, the law of gravity, and the law of GOYA, they combine to drive the law of allowance: You will ultimately reap what you sow. When you project your goals into the world with intention, resist gravity without getting discouraged, and work hard, you will harvest good results, at the appropriate time during your unique journey.

If you have faith in these laws, take action to practice them, and stay patient, they will work their magic. The results you seek will start to follow.

2

Victim, Survivor, or Conqueror?

YOU MIGHT HEAR SOME complicated theories about different mindsets, but to me there are only three basic ones: victim, survivor, and conqueror. The one you choose will give you very different ways of reacting and responding to adversity.

I've seen the victim mindset in a surprising number of people who go into sales. They always deny it, due to their lack of self-awareness. But the dead giveaway is that people with a victim mindset always self-justify when something goes wrong. They never take responsibility for any problems.

When I managed reps who thought like victims, they'd say, "I can't hit my sales targets because . . ." and the reason was always something external. Maybe they didn't have enough training. Or the product was bad, or too expensive. Or the neighborhood sucked, or the list of leads they were given had no potential. Or the sales script wasn't effective. No matter what the excuse, there was never even a dim awareness that maybe they needed to study more, practice more, work harder, and take responsibility for their own performance.

I'd reply that other reps (myself included) were doing far better with the exact same training, products, neighborhoods, leads, and scripts. In fact, some of us were killing it. If all those factors were really the problem, the company would be going out of business instead of thriving. So I'd say, "Maybe, just maybe, this might be a you problem rather than a company problem." Sometimes I'd knock doors with them for a few hours in the same neighborhood, just to show what was possible if they'd stop thinking like victims and work on their self-development.

The survivor mindset is one step up from the victim, because survivors do take personal responsibility. As a result they get better outcomes than victims. But the big problem for survivors is that they set the bar too low. They focus on the bare minimum required to meet their basic needs, and if they hit that number, they're happy. Survivors struggle with ambition and can't seem to imagine a bigger vision of what's possible.

A typical survivor sales rep will first look at his basic needs, which I call a *nut*. Let's say he's young and single, and every month he spends $1,000 on rent, $500 on a car payment, $500 on groceries and utilities, and $1,000 for everything else, including fun. That's a $3,000 nut, which adds up to $36,000 a year after taxes. If this survivor can make $45,000 after taxes, he can cover his nut and save a little for the future, and he'll feel good about it. If he breaks $50,000, he'll feel like a rock star. In other words he's not dreaming big, or even dreaming medium.

Now imagine that this survivor gets on a hot streak one quarter and nets $25,000—double his usual commissions. It's the best quarter of his life, and he's thrilled. But instead of seeing this as a floor for what's possible in the future, he sees it as a ceiling. He starts to get complacent, because he's already covered $25K of his $36K annual nut, so he feels like he can take things easy for a while. Maybe he'll put in fewer hours, or sell with less intensity. He'll try to coast on that burst of success without downgrading his lifestyle.

This kind of complacency will do almost as much damage as a victim mentality. If you're just doing enough to survive, you won't come anywhere close to approaching the true limits of your potential.

The third mindset type, the conqueror, neither blames the world for failures nor defines success as merely getting by. He's looking to compete and excel. He thinks, *If that guy is making X, I bet I can do even better.* If the company record for monthly sales is $300,000, the conqueror is gunning to break it. He's always looking for the next hill to climb. It's not even mostly about the money—it's about the excitement of setting a big goal and then nailing it. After that, the conqueror will set another big goal, because that adrenaline rush is addictive.

But there's a downside of the conqueror mentality that I call a *success void.* After every hill you climb, you start back at the bottom of another hill, maybe a bigger hill. And you might have a moment of thinking, *Oh crap! Now what?* If your greatest happiness comes from conquering, you might start to think you suck if you ever stop conquering.

What will happen if you eventually slow down, make less money, maybe get out of shape and lose your youthful good looks? Will everyone in your life abandon you? A conqueror needs to make time for family and friends and other sources of joy, not just setting new personal bests.

I used to be the number-one sales rep at one of the largest direct-to-consumer companies in the country, Vivint. One year the company gave me a huge trophy at the annual awards meeting—it must have weighed fifty pounds. But as I walked up for the presentation, I looked at the crowd and I could tell that nobody really gave a crap. I got some congratulations and some polite applause, but then it was on to the next people getting other awards. I had to wrestle with the truth that being number one is great, but it's not everything.

I still think the conqueror mindset is by far the best. You should definitely be looking for mountains to climb. You should maximize every ounce of your potential. But that mindset can fill in only part of the puzzle of success and happiness. You also have to learn to love yourself and other people, and make time for everything else that's also super important. We'll return to that theme later in the book.

3

Would You Rather Be a W-2 or a 1099?

THERE ARE TWO BASIC KINDS of relationships between a worker and an employer. The tax jargon is W-2 versus 1099, but the difference goes way beyond taxes.*

If you work for wages or a salary, every year the company sends you a W-2 statement that you have to file with your federal taxes. It means you're being paid for your *time*, whether by the hour, the week, or the year.

If you're an independent contractor, you get a 1099 statement instead of a W-2. This means you're being paid not for your time but for the *value* you bring to the company, through sales commissions or other fees.

The herbivore mindset is that it's safer to be a W-2, paid for your time. It's predictable and consistent. Maybe your job comes with medical insurance, a 401(k) plan, or other benefits. Those things may not add up to a lot, but at least you know what you're getting, even if you just do the bare minimum expected. Of course, that's assuming you don't get fired or laid off.

The carnivore mindset is that it's better to be a 1099, paid for your value. That's riskier because if you don't generate value, you won't get

---

* Please note that nothing in this chapter should be taken as tax advice or legal advice.

paid anything. And you won't get insurance, a 401(k), paid vacation time, etc.

But the upside of a 1099 career is unlimited potential. You eat what you kill, so you can control how much you need to work or want to work to reach your goals. You control how much vacation time you can take. You never have to beg your boss for a day off. You won't be trapped in the permanent grind, working sixty plus hours a week for fifty weeks a year, if you can make the money you need in less time. In short, a 1099 gives you both maximum freedom and a maximum incentive to work hard and make the most of every hour you put in.

For most of our grandparents, a steady paycheck was a badge of honor and success. But now it can easily become a trap that keeps you from approaching your true earning potential. A W-2 person can fall into the mindset of depending on their boss or company to set up the conditions for success, such as providing strong inbound sales leads. That kind of dependency can make you feel helpless, like you can't succeed unless someone else does the prospecting for you.

In contrast, a 1099 person is usually generating their own leads. Hunting for prospects. Being creative. Solving problems. Betting on themselves. Not waiting around for anyone's help.

When I got recruited to be the VP of sales at Solcius, they told me it was a W-2 position with a good base salary, but a cap on commissions. I replied, "Hell no! I want to be commission only, and I want to make you write such huge commission checks that you'll be crying. I want to be the highest earner at this company!"

The CEO looked at me like I was crazy as I pitched my counteroffer.

"The more I sell and the more my team sells, the more you make, right? So why would you want to put a cap on how much you make?"

I then explained two other nonnegotiable conditions, on top of being a 1099.

First, they had to agree in writing that they wouldn't punish me or try to change my commission if I made way more than everybody else in this company. "My last company freaked out because I was making too much money and creating too many new customers for them to process. So they fired me. I can't have that again."

Second, they also had to agree that it was the company's responsibility to ramp up operations to handle all the business I was about to generate. "I can't have customers complaining that it's taking them weeks or months to get installations or get their loans approved. I'm going to close more deals faster than anyone you've worked with before. If my customers get pissed off at processing delays, that's bad for all of us. So you have to hire as many installation crews and loan processors as it takes to keep up."

Solcius agreed to those terms, and the result was a big win-win for all of us.

These days, as the CEO of my own company, I see the difference between W-2 people and 1099 people from the other side of the desk. Whenever we post openings for salespeople, some applicants would rather have a reliable five-figure salary than the opportunity to make far more, but without the security of a steady paycheck.

I like to say to potential new sales reps for my company, "We have two different compensation options. One is a W-2 with a modest base salary plus a small commission. You'll probably make between sixty and eighty grand a year, and we'll add you to our group health insurance. The other is a 1099 arrangement with zero base salary and no benefits, but a much bigger commission per sale. If you're good, you can make several hundred thousand per year, and if you're great, you might make seven figures. Which one sounds better to you?"

If the job applicant is more interested in the W-2 option, I know that person isn't a carnivore.

If you have the courage to bet on yourself, to be a self-starter, to eat what you kill, 1099 is clearly the way to go. Otherwise you might be dooming yourself to a life of underperformance and frustration.

4

The Mental Governor

A GOLF CART GOES SLOWLY because it has a device called a governor that limits the highest possible speed the motor can generate. It's a safety feature to prevent knucklehead golfers from racing around in their carts and getting injured. I know that because I was one of those knuckleheads! A friend once showed me a simple trick to disable the governor, so I floored it. It was a lot of fun to be flying down the fairway . . . until I hit a bump and the cart flipped over. Nearly killed myself!

After that I started to appreciate the value of a golf cart governor. And it occurred to me that many salespeople have a governor on their mindset that artificially limits their performance. That one isn't a safety feature—it's a serious problem.

I define a mental governor as a false belief about what a salesperson's maximum output can and should be. If this belief takes hold, their subconscious mind steers them to stay under that artificial limit. But just like with a golf cart, it's possible to disable a mental governor. Once you do, there's almost no limit on how much you can accomplish.

The mental governor usually comes from other people talking about average numbers, such as average closings per week or average commissions per rep. It's very easy for your subconscious to hear *average* and translate it to "my goal" or "what's expected" or even "success." I learned that the hard way at age eighteen.

Do you remember the story I told you about my first grown-up job with Platinum Protection? I was right out of high school and had just landed in Dallas for the first time. Didn't know anyone in town or anything about alarm systems. The sales manager, Luke, had me shadow him for a couple of hours that Friday afternoon while he knocked doors. Then he left me with a packet of product information, the standard pitch, the closing process, three blank contracts, and instructions on which streets to hit the next day.

So picture this. It's Saturday morning, my first day on the job, and I'm on my own. About an hour after I start knocking, I call Luke because I'm closing my first sale, and some of the paperwork is confusing. I'm not sure how to fill in some of the blanks. He walks me through it on the phone, and my customer signs the contract.

A couple of hours later, around lunchtime, I call my manager again. "Hey, Luke, do you have any more of those blank contracts?"

He says, "Why, did you mess them up?"

"No—you only gave me three, and I just closed my third customer. So I need more for the rest of the day."

He sounds surprised, so I ask how many he's sold so far today. Just one. I figure that's because he must be busy doing manager stuff, not just knocking doors. He drives to where I am in the neighborhood and gives me some more blank contracts.

That Monday at the team meeting, all the sales reps report their numbers for Saturday. Luke goes down the whiteboard with all our names on it, asking how many deals we closed. The answers called out are something like "One . . . zero . . . three . . . one . . . zero . . . two . . . zero . . . two . . . one . . ."

He gets to me last because I'm the new guy; my name is at the bottom of the whiteboard. I say, "Five," and everyone stops and stares at me. I'm eighteen, selling alarm systems for the first time, and I closed five deals on my first day? *Really?* So I ask what's normal, and someone says, "If you can average one close per day, that's awesome."

Until that moment, I didn't have a mental governor for this job. I had no idea what normal was, so I just sold as many as I could, as fast as I could. But now that I know the average, it messes with my head. I end up closing only five customers for that entire week, Monday through Saturday. Average, not great. Not really even good.

This happens all the time when people benchmark against the average. When you start working, someone tells you that a good job pays $75K a year and a great job pays $100K, and those numbers become your governor. Or you hear that the average D2D sales rep makes $43K a year, and that gets stuck in your head.

Or maybe you work backwards from your expenses, like the folks we discussed who have a survivor mindset. You do some basic monthly budget math—X for rent, Y for food, Z for a car payment, and $1,500 for fun and to save for a down payment on a house. Then you know the minimum you need to cover that nut, which becomes your mental governor.

But this kind of thinking is bogus. Why try to earn the average for your company, or the whole industry, when you can aim for whatever the top 1 percent of performers are making? Why just aim to cover your expenses, when you might have the capacity to blow past your current expenses and change your whole quality of life?

You have to take the mental governor off your goals. Tell yourself that you don't want to play it safe—you want to floor it and see how fast the golf cart can go. You won't know until you really try, with no preconceived limit. And unlike me, you can't actually flip your cart over!

This is not to say benchmarking is worthless. But if you feel like you have to benchmark, look at the top 1 percent of your peers, not the folks in the middle of the bell curve. Forget about those average folks.

This can be a hard mindset shift for a lot of us, if our parents taught us that being average at anything is good enough. If your parents felt satisfied with their $60K or $75K jobs, you might feel disrespectful to start aiming for $200K or $500K or seven figures. In my case, my benchmark from high school was painting street addresses on curbs for $20 a pop, and grossing $120 was a five-star day. But now I was a full-time D2D professional selling a serious product, and I had to ditch my old benchmark.

Carnivores never accept average as their goal. You have to take off the mental governor and find out what's really possible.

5

Activate Your Prey Drive

MY FRIEND COACH BERT taught me the concept of "prey drive"—not *pray* but *prey*, as in the smaller, slower animals hunted by lions and tigers. Humans have an instinct to hunt, just like predatory animals. But unlike lions and tigers, sometimes our natural instincts get jammed up instead of kicking in. We lose our killer instinct. If that happens, we need to activate our prey drive to go back on the hunt.

When your prey drive is firing on all cylinders, it gives you persistence and intensity. *Persistence* means showing up every day, with a commitment to moving relentlessly in the right direction, until you get where you want to go. It's getting back up after you get knocked down, every single time. *Intensity* means an intentional application of force, power, and ferocity of attack. Combined, persistence and intensity are unstoppable, like a tiger that won't stop until it chases down a smaller animal.

There are five reliable ways to activate that prey drive—to give it a jump start if it seems to be stuck:

1. Competition
2. Fear of loss
3. Inspiration by others
4. Environment
5. Public exposure

Competition can be as simple as tracking the results of the other reps at your company and setting out to beat them. At one of my early jobs selling alarm systems, I started dead last out of about thirty reps, because I had joined late in the season and all the others had a two-month head start. Seeing my name at the bottom of the results board triggered my competitive instinct. Every day when I went out to knock doors, I could visualize where I was on that board and who was directly ahead of me. I got more fired up by the chance to move up than by my commissions.

The following week I was higher on the list, and there were two new names directly above mine, so I focused on displacing those guys. That process repeated each week as I climbed up the board. Other people noticed that the new guy was rising, which motivated them in return. By the end of the season I had cracked the top five, despite starting two months late. My competitiveness and sense of personal pride were a huge motivating force.

Fear of loss is simple: if you don't achieve X, something bad will happen. You don't need an external authority figure to set up a loss—you can do it yourself. For instance, here's a hack I used when I was trying to break my sugar addiction. I told my assistant that I'd pay her $1,000 if she ever saw me eating sugary foods between Monday and Friday. Soon after, she saw me drinking kombucha—I thought it was healthy and had no idea that it contained something like twenty-eight grams of sugar. So I had to Venmo her $1,000, which really stung. In the moment, day to day, that loss was a stronger motivator than my long-term goal of getting in awesome shape.

You can adapt this to your sales goals by setting a clear negative incentive to create a fear of loss. Let's say you have a strong desire to vacation in Hawaii in the winter. But you tell yourself, your friends, and your significant other that you won't even plan the trip unless you close one hundred sales that year. Doesn't matter if your friends are going, or if you have enough money to take that vacation even if you close just eighty sales. It has to be one hundred, or no Hawaii. Now the fear of loss will activate your prey drive—especially if a failure will mean disappointing your spouse and family, not just yourself.

Inspiration by others is a way to fire up your prey drive by hunting alongside the best hunters you can find. If you reach out to the best salespeople in your field and ask permission to ride along, watch and learn, you will start to think like those elite performers. You'll feel a hunger to play at their level—because if they can do it, why can't you? Seek out people who inspire you, and do everything in your power to spend more time with them.

Environment is the flip side of inspiration. Just as hanging out with high performers will motivate you to become a high performer, a mediocre peer group will subconsciously drag you down. If you hang around salespeople who put in an average effort and are happy with average results, as long as they can go home early and watch lots of Netflix, there's a good chance you'll become one of them. You may need to pull away from their negative influence, even if that means losing them as friends. It's sad but true: if you want to excel, you may need to delete certain people from your environment.

Public exposure is the flip side of competition. Remember that job where they posted the whole team's sales numbers every week, for the whole company to see? I used that results board as a positive, as competitive fuel, but others saw it as a terrifying threat. Their nightmare was having their peers and bosses find out that they had a terrible week, with zero sales closed. Public exposure was strong motivation to get off their asses every day and really focus.

Those are your five main activators of prey drive. The more of them you can build into your daily work, the more relentless and fired up you'll be. Think about ways you can change your systems and practices to incorporate at least two or three.

By the way, did you notice what's *not* on the list of the five activators? Prizes and bonuses. Some sales managers think they can turn people around with a hundred-dollar bonus for hitting a certain level of sales per week. Or they might offer a gift card to some store, or a fancy restaurant. That's all low-level stuff, and it can't compete with the self-pride that underlies the five activators. An extra hundred dollars is nice, but not even remotely as cool as going home to your spouse and proudly announcing how many deals you closed.

Feeling like a winner is priceless. Focus on the mindset hacks that will make you feel like a winner.

6

Just One More Door

THIS IS ONE OF the most powerful mental hacks I've discovered, and it works for any kind of sales. Before you end a workday or a shift, tell yourself, *Just one more door* or *Just one more call*. Instead of knocking off a little early, stay a little late. You'll feel like you ended on a high note, which will make you feel better about the day and eager to come back tomorrow.

Let's say I'm knocking doors and my shift is supposed to end at 8:00 p.m. I finish at a prospect's house at 7:50. I could stop at that point and head for my car, because it's so close to eight. No one, even my boss, is going to give me a hard time for ending ten minutes early. Otherwise I might end up talking to my next prospect until 8:30 or even 9:00, which would really cut into my evening.

But if I start cutting out at 7:50, the next night it might be 7:45, which is basically the same. Then 7:30. Then 7:00. Over time, this "knock off early" mindset would escalate, and my results would drift downward.

But what if, instead of winding down a little early, I tell myself, "Just one more door." I psych myself up again and knock at a new house. If it works and I'm busy closing a deal for another hour, that's not a problem—it's a win! And even if that last pitch of the day doesn't work, I'll still feel good because I finished strong.

It's the same concept as running through the finish line. If you've ever run competitively, you've heard a coach tell you *not* to slow down as you approach the finish line. You're supposed to keep running as fast as possible. Momentum will carry you past the finish line—maybe five feet past, maybe twenty—but that's *good*. You want to cross the line with a final burst of energy so you'll feel like you really did your best and left it all on the track.

If you add one or even two extra pitches every evening before you go home, that might add up to a few hundred extra prospects per year—prospects you otherwise wouldn't be talking to at all. Depending on your closing ratio, that might mean dozens of additional closed sales over that year. And that will translate into exponentially more income than another rep who's equally talented but goes home at 7:50. It's a difference in mindset, not skill. And the impact of this difference will compound over time, as "just one more door" becomes an automatic habit.

What really matters isn't what time you stop working; it's about what you've accomplished that day. My goal is to maximize my closed deals every single day. Knocking just one more door is a proven way to do that. So it doesn't feel like self-punishment; it feels like an extra opportunity.

It's not that I *have to* knock one more door—I'm grateful to have the *opportunity* to knock one more door. That's the mindset of a consistently top-tier performer.

7
Carnivores Do Best in Packs

IF YOU'RE A CARNIVORE or aspiring carnivore, you'll do even better if you find a team of salespeople with the same eat-what-you-kill mindset. Carnivores, like wolves, perform best in packs. There's nothing like the camaraderie of a kick-ass team to keep you fired up, feeling confident, and constantly improving your skills. You'll develop the sense that, as a pack, you're unstoppable. And you'll be reminded that there are plenty of opportunities for everyone in the pack to be fully satisfied. It's much harder to stay motivated and at the top of your game as a lone wolf.

But if you're the weakest member of your pack, watch out. You will have to raise your game and keep up with the alpha wolves, or else you'll have to leave to find another pack. Your pack won't want to keep you around if you're bringing down their overall performance.

I learned a lot about team dynamics when I started managing D2D sales teams for Vivint. I was the designated driver for four or five people when we canvassed a new neighborhood. I'd drive everyone to a central point in the morning, and then we'd continue on foot to the different streets we were each assigned. The plan was to meet back at the car at night, usually 9:00 pm. We were like Special Forces dropped behind enemy lines. We trained and prepared as a team, but we each ate what we killed as individuals.

When people on my team were going through a cold streak,

they'd often call me in the middle of the day for help. "Sam, I keep striking out, can you come knock with me for a while?"

I learned to reply, "No, because that won't do either of us any good. I need to knock on my own doors, and you need to practice until you get better. You can come with me for a while and watch me knock, if you think that will help, but it won't make you any money today."

Sometimes the calls and texts I got were increasingly desperate.

"Sam, can you drive me to a gas station to buy water?"

"Sam, I'm starving, I haven't eaten all day, can you get me something?"

"Sam, I really need a bathroom, can you take me to one?"

As much as I might be tempted to drop everything to give someone a ride, I learned that it wouldn't solve their problems. First, by that point I was averaging around $800 an hour, so wasting a half hour to drive another rep to a gas station was basically $400 out of my own pocket. But more important, they had to learn self-reliance.

So I'd reply something like "Don't panic, everything you need is right in front of you. There are three hundred houses in your zone today. Behind those three hundred doors are a lot of nice people who will let you use their bathroom. They'll offer you a glass of water or a banana. And beyond that, your income is behind those three hundred doors. Your future is behind those three hundred doors. So you need to practice getting through those doors!"

Because of this tough love, carnivores appreciated being assigned to my car, and herbivores hated it. New reps either loved the energy and sales tips they got as part of my team, or felt outclassed and overwhelmed. They either rose to the challenge or went somewhere else. At the end of each day of knocking, when we met up again at the car, some would look upbeat and energized by their successes. Others looked completely defeated, like they had been physically beaten up.

We had an informal contest to see who would show up at the car last because their final pitch of the day extended past the meeting time. Because I was the top-performing rep, that was often me. Sometimes I wouldn't even knock my last door until 9:00, while others were already walking back to the car. And if my last pitch went well, it might take me ninety minutes or even two hours to close and get the paperwork filled out.

Meanwhile everyone else was just waiting at the car for their ride home, which might be an hour away. Sometimes they didn't get home before midnight. I'm sure some of them hated my guts on nights like that, when they got a text from me that I'd just started a presentation at 9:00.

But I didn't tolerate much complaining. I'd say something like "Look, we're all here to close as many deals as possible. Tomorrow you could be the one doing a final knock at nine and not finishing till ten thirty, and I'd respect that and feel happy for you. I want to get home just as much as you do, but I focus on why we're here. So instead of complaining about me, think about how you can beat me to become the one who keeps everyone else waiting."

Some of them embraced that mindset and wanted to learn every detail of what I was doing. They grasped that the "just one more door" strategy we covered in the last chapter, when compounded over an entire year, could pay off with a ton of extra income.

Others, unfortunately, never caught on to that mindset. They kept cutting out as early as they could get away with. And they didn't stay in our pack for too long.

8

Salesnertia

YOU MAY KNOW THAT inertia is a law of physics that says any object at rest stays at rest, and any object in motion stays in motion, until some force changes it. Salesnertia simply applies that law to sales: A salesperson on the couch stays on the couch, and a salesperson who gets on a roll will stay on a roll.

The way you start each day or each shift sets the tone for everything that follows, good or bad. So you have to make an intentional effort to start strong. I call it running to your first door, but it also applies to your first cold call or your first scheduled meeting. Get pumped, move your body around, get to wherever you need to be, and then make that first pitch with extra energy. This will start your momentum for the next few hours. Your brain and body run on inertia.

If you have the power to set your own hours, start early! An early first appointment or first call will set the ball rolling for the whole day. But a light or empty morning can leave you just puttering around until lunchtime and then dragging all afternoon. Hit the ground running!

If you hit a rough patch later in the day and feel your momentum draining, take a few minutes to stretch and move around again. Physical movement can break a mental logjam. Once you start moving, it's easier to start talking. Conversely, the worst thing you can do is melt into a couch, your comfy office chair, or your car seat. Maybe you assume that taking a break to check Instagram or ESPN.com will recharge your brain, but it will just redirect your momentum in the totally wrong direction.

One fast way to kick-start your salesnertia is a trick I've taught to a lot of door knockers. I call it a *turfie*—a selfie taken in the turf where you're supposed to be knocking doors. Let's say your shift is supposed to start at 2:00 p.m. A couple of minutes before two, get out of your car and take a turfie of yourself, as you're about to knock on the first door of your shift. Text that picture to a friend who can act as your accountability partner. The message is *I'm here, I'm ready to go, let's do this*.

Once you're in positive motion, you won't go back to your car to hide. You'll keep moving forward. You'll knock that first door and get on a roll for the rest of your shift.

If your whole team gets into the same pattern of good habits—starting early, ramping up energy, sharing turfies in a group text chat—each individual's salesnertia will reinforce the whole team's momentum and overall performance. It's a powerful mindset hack.

Bottom line: Action leads to more action. Salesnertia—your own and your team's—breeds more salesnertia. Whenever you feel stuck, force yourself back into action.

9

The Greatest Competition Is with Yourself

DID YOU KNOW THAT LeBron James spends about $1 million a year of his own money on improving his fitness and conditioning? Personal trainers and nutritionists help him stay elite and become even more elite. He doesn't have to do that—he'd still be amazing just by training like a typical NBA starter. But because he *does* do it, he's not typical—he's LeBron.

Michael Jordan and Kobe Bryant had the same carnivore mindset: always focused on reaching and then surpassing the absolute peak of their potential, not coasting on their past glory. I met the man who trained both of them, Tim Grover, at one of my conferences. Michael and Kobe saw hiring a superstar trainer like Tim as an investment, worth every penny.

Another way to think of it is that LeBron, Michael, and Kobe all saw their greatest competition as themselves, not their teammates or even their opponents. When the average NBA starter has a twenty-point game, he's stoked, because that's way better than the league average of nine to eleven points per game. After a twenty-point game, most players feel like buying everyone a round of drinks and calling their parents with pride.

But the truly elite players, the top 1 percent of the league, aren't stoked by a twenty-point game. They're *pissed*. They know they can do better. They don't care if they had the high score of the game—

that's irrelevant. If their all-time career high is thirty-five points, they say why not forty? Or fifty? That's the mindset they bring on the court every night.

Suppose you find out that the average D2D rep in your field closes one sale per day. If you have a two-close day, you might be thrilled. But I'm sure the top 1 percent in your world (the sales equivalent of LeBron or Kobe) won't be celebrating a two-close day. They know they can close three, four, five, maybe more. They're aiming for the far-right tail of the bell curve, not the fat part in the middle. They're competing with their own potential.

Of course, some people think this mindset is a great way to make yourself crazy and miserable. Why beat yourself up over a twenty-point game or a two-close day, when nearly everyone else would be celebrating? The answer goes back to what we said about survivor versus conqueror: Why aim for just enough success to get by, when you could be aiming to join the top 1 percent? You won't find out how high you can climb unless you benchmark against your own potential, not anyone else's.

THIS RELATES TO a concept I call *taking shelter in statistics*. Imagine a company with twenty sales reps. The top two make more than $100,000 in commissions, and the other eighteen make somewhere between $40,000 and $70,000. If your commissions come in at $60,000, you can tell yourself that you're doing pretty well, compared with most of the team. Those top two guys must be freaks of nature, or maybe they're cheating somehow to get better leads. Either way, it's easy to think that you can ignore those two outliers.

Now imagine that you sell for the same company, but this time eighteen of the twenty reps are making above $100K. In this scenario your $60K makes you feel like an outlier—a failure. Same product, same boss, same commissions, but a different benchmark. It changes your whole self-perception, right?

Don't take shelter in how your stats compare with the average rep. You *want* to be the outlier, on the high side. You *want* to be the one whose results leave average reps mystified. There's nothing that the top 1 percent are achieving that you can't also achieve. Don't let the average pull you down; that's the road to permanent mediocrity. You're not trying to be an "overachiever," because that word implies valuing yourself against everyone else. Just aim to be the best achiever you can possibly be. Other people's results are their business, not yours.

BACK WHEN I WAS the new guy at my first alarm systems company, I had a total bagel of a Saturday—zero closes after a full day of knocking. That night all the reps on my team went to a Buffalo Wild Wings to hang out. The ones who'd had a great day were celebrating and buying rounds of drinks.

But I didn't feel like celebrating. In fact, I felt so terrible that I went outside the restaurant and called my mom. "Last Saturday I closed five sales, but today I did zero. This sucks! This was the hardest effing day of my life! I don't know what's wrong with me!" I was close to tears. Mom replied something like "Nothing is wrong with you! You just had a bad day. Taggarts don't quit. Get back out there, you little turd!"

So I went back inside with my team. And it hit me that the other guys who had struck out all day, or even all week, were having a great time, like nothing was wrong. Not only were they not as upset as I was, they didn't seem bothered at all. Yet some of them hadn't made a dime all week!

I eventually realized that it was healthy for me to get upset when I underperformed, as long as I didn't give up. Michael Jordan and

LeBron James got upset on their bad days—they never pretended that it didn't matter. They got angry at themselves, then tried to figure out what had gone wrong. Then they got back out there the next day. That's what carnivores and conquerors do.

If you ever reach the point where you're the best salesperson on your team, or in your whole company, those colleagues can easily become your new mental governor. They might be the ones holding you back or even pulling you backwards, if you're just trying to fit in instead of reaching your full potential. Don't fall into that trap!

It feels like a paradox, but true masters in any field never feel like they've reached total mastery. No matter how high they've already climbed, they're still hungry for more knowledge, skills, and insights to get even better. They never stop trying to improve, no matter how many points, victories, or championships they already have, or who is telling them they're already the best, or how much money they're making.

I want to work with people who see their only true competition as their own prior personal bests.

I want to be friends with people who *never* stop their journey of self-improvement.

10

Impeccable Integrity

THIS IS A STORY I rarely tell, because it's embarrassing. It's from about ten years ago, when I was the number-one D2D rep for Vivint, selling alarm systems.

One day I go out to knock doors in a tiny rural town in Texas, truly in the middle of nowhere. The kind of area where door knockers are rare and a whole block is immediately on guard as soon as an unknown car parks in front of someone's house. I grew up in an area like that in Utah. We used to give out big candy bars at Halloween because we'd get only about three kids doing trick-or-treat, so my mom figured we might as well be generous.

I go up to a door and pitch the homeowner. He tells me his house is next door to his cousin's house, and they've combined their backyards into one big backyard with a shared pool. He invites me to the backyard so I can meet the cousin too. After a long conversation by the pool, I close both of them on new alarm systems with five-year monitoring contracts. It's a great day for me already.

But when I look at the paperwork the next morning, I realize that I got a signature on the contract of only one of the cousins. The other guy agreed verbally but never signed his contract. This means I have to drive back out to the middle of nowhere just for a signature, killing three hours of prime selling time. I really don't want to do that, so I just sign the guy's name and process the paperwork. It doesn't feel dishonest because I'm giving him the exact terms he agreed to.

No one might have ever noticed, except that the technicians who install the alarms accidentally break the guy's doorjamb and leave without fixing it. The guy calls our customer service department to complain. No response. He keeps calling for weeks and getting the runaround, because they're too backed up to send someone out to his house to fix it.

Finally he calls customer service one more time. "It's been three months, and I can't even close my door because your guy messed it up. I want to cancel my contract." Customer service says he can't cancel because of the fine print in his contract, and they email him a scan of it. The guy looks at it and says that's not his signature.

Oh crap.

Soon after, my manager calls me to ask what the hell happened, and I explain it. He then calls back with a lawyer from our legal department. The lawyer says I committed forgery, which is a felony. So not only am I about to get fired, I might go to prison. I start shaking and thinking, *How am I gonna tell my wife? How did I just go from being the number-one rep at this company to a potential felon?* I ask for the chance to try to fix things with the customer before they have me arrested.

I call the guy and apologize sincerely. He's angry, of course. But he also remembers how much he liked me that day when we were hanging out in his backyard with his cousin.

I say, "Listen, I'm going to pay off your entire monitoring contract for all five years. The monitoring is on me. And of course we're going to get your doorjamb fixed right away. All I'm asking in return is, can you sign a new contract so we can put this behind us?" He agrees, and I drive back out there with a tech to watch the repair and get the guy's signature. I don't go to prison and don't even get fired.

That experience has stuck with me ever since. Integrity isn't something you can mess around with. Even the smallest bending of the rules can lead to a catastrophe, not just for one rep but for a whole company. You can't take that kind of risk. If this customer hadn't liked me enough to take pity on me, my whole life would have been screwed up.

From then on I committed to doing sales with impeccable integrity. I don't push the limits anymore, even a little bit. I don't lie to prospects, even a little bit. I definitely don't commit forgery just to avoid three hours of driving.

I believe in taking risks, but some risks are just dumb.

11

You Might Be Saving a Life

IN ADDITION TO FOCUSING on helping your customers, you can also tell yourself that you might even be saving their lives. This mindset hack is not as crazy as you might think.

When I was a kid in a small town in Utah, we almost never locked our front and back doors. Crime just wasn't a concern. If anyone had knocked to try to sell us an alarm system, my parents would have just laughed. I was taught to assume the best about most people and not fear our neighbors.

So it was a culture shock when I started selling alarm systems and learned how to talk about break-ins. At first I didn't want to frighten potential customers. But at some point I realized, no one can predict what's going to happen. Every day in this country, even in peaceful towns, people have their houses broken into. Or they have fires start while everyone is asleep. Or they have some other kind of crisis where an alarm system might save lives.

I started thinking that if I fail to close someone and then they got broken into or had a fire, it was basically my fault. I could have protected them if I had sold them better. A botched sale didn't just mean a lost commission—maybe it would mean an innocent person injured or dead, or losing a loved one or valuable property. So I started to reframe my pitch:

Would you rather close the gate before the horse is out, or after?

Why not do something to protect your family that doesn't cost much in the long run?

I hope you will never need this system, but I want you to sleep better because you have it. If you can sleep better, I'll sleep a little better too.

I tried out this angle in the small town of Canadian, Texas. It reminded me of where I grew up—about two thousand people who all know each other, with virtually no break-ins in living memory. Most people in town didn't even bother locking their doors, so other reps felt like selling alarm systems there was like selling sand on Miami Beach. But my pitch was working! I sold a system to a local cop and the principal at the high school. Then I sold a woman who knew everyone in town, a type I call Nosy Nancy.

Soon enough, when I knocked on a new door, I could show this list of other customers in town who were getting our alarm system, which added social proof. People felt more comfortable getting an alarm system, knowing that the cop and the principal thought it was a good idea.

Then I got to an older dude who lived by himself and was skeptical about the need for security. He said he felt totally capable of defending his home if necessary. I said, "I believe you, but what if you have a medical emergency? What if you fall and break something? You're too far away for your neighbors to hear you yelling. I would feel terrible if you died because I failed to give you this protection."

After about a two-hour conversation, I sold him our medical alert pendant with monitoring. Then I left and forgot about him. He was just one of a hundred sales I closed that year.

About a year later I was back in that same town to do another round of knocking. A woman opened her door and said, after I barely started talking, "Hold on, are you the guy who was here last year?" Then she started crying. I remember thinking, *I've had people yell at me and cuss at me and try to kick me in the nuts, but no one has ever started crying when I started a sales pitch.*

Then she explained that her father was the skeptical man who kept me talking for two hours before buying the medical alert system. A few months after that, he fell and broke his hip, and the only way he could get help was pushing his medical alert button. It literally saved his life.

Then she asked me to go to his house with her to surprise him. I thought that was weird. I could barely remember the guy, and I didn't want to waste time while I still had a bunch of doors to knock. But I said sure, let's go. When we got there and he saw me, he started crying, too, thanking me over and over. We hugged and took pictures together.

Then it hit me: The six years I sold alarm systems was totally worth it, if only for this family. Yes the money was great, but here was proof that I saved at least one life. I bet I also saved other people I'd never hear about. Who knows how many break-ins got stopped, how many fires got put out before they did serious damage? Those people would never bother to call their sales rep, but they were out there!

That became part of my mindset ever since.

You can embrace the same mindset even if your product or service isn't as obviously protective as an alarm system. If you sell cars, the safety features on a new model might save a life. If you sell solar, a family's cost savings might make a huge impact on their budget. You'll never know for sure, but you'll get an energy boost if you assume your work is changing lives. Maybe even saving them.

12

Everything Is Sales

I'M ALWAYS A LITTLE SURPRISED when people say they have no interest in sales, or that sales isn't relevant to their career. Don't they realize that *everything* is sales? If you want to get literally anything, in either your work life or your personal life, you need to become decent at sales. Opportunities to hone your skills come up every day.

Not long ago I was at a conference and brought my own health-food package that needed to be microwaved. I went to the concession stand and asked one of the workers, "Hey, could you do me a favor and throw this in the microwave in the back?"

The dude looked at me and said flatly, "No, we don't do that."

"But do you have a microwave, right?"

"Yeah, but we can't just take your stuff and put it in. That's against the rules."

I looked at him for a second and I could tell he wasn't going to budge. So I walked a little farther down and looked at some of the other workers. I picked out a young woman who seemed friendly and went over to her. "Excuse me, I have a huge favor to ask. I need this special food and it has to be microwaved. I know you're not supposed to, but could you have a heart and pop this in your microwave for a minute?" And she did.

The next day at the same conference, I was in the middle of an important conversation during the lunch break, so I asked one of my colleagues to get my health food microwaved. She was gone for twenty minutes, then came back and said she had walked around to different locations, but none of them were able to do it.

So I went back with her to one of those concession locations, and as a test I walked into the area through the side door, the staff only door. Two of the workers glared at me and came at me like bulls, because I had to get out of their workspace. But the third guy was chill about it—he just smiled. And I knew immediately, *that's my guy*. It didn't take a PhD in psychology to read those reactions.

A minute later I walked up to the third guy's spot at the counter. "Hey, man, can you do me a huge solid and throw this in the microwave for a minute? I'd really appreciate it." And he did.

As we were walking back to our table, my colleague made a comment about how charming I was and how easy it was for me to get people to do things. I said it's not charm, or at least not mostly. It's sales skills that anyone can learn.

I started with a positive mindset: *I can do this.*

I scouted for the right prospect.

I stayed resilient when the first couple of prospects didn't show any promise.

I figured out how to get on the third guy's good side.

I made a pitch that he couldn't resist, to help a stranger even though it was against the rules.

Then I closed the "sale" and got my meal microwaved!

The result was success in five minutes rather than failure in twenty minutes. Not due to charm or luck, but by recognizing that everything is sales. Sales skills can be applied to a huge range of everyday situations.

There's no need to get indignant with people, to hear "No" from a worker and demand to talk to their manager. There's no need to raise a stink or threaten anyone. That's a victim mentality. You'll get so much more of what you want if you can play these situations smart rather than angry.

13

Burnout Is a Mindset Problem

HOW DO YOU THINK ABOUT your work time versus your downtime? Obviously we all need downtime for food and sleep and fun and seeing our loved ones. But do you start each workday like a fully charged phone, or a half-charged phone? Then does everything you do at work drain your power?

Most salespeople—the herbivores—think their work is draining, so they're always looking for opportunities to plug in their batteries for a recharge. They tend to ask their managers, *When's my lunch break? When's my fifteen-minute break?* But in reality, those breaks aren't doing much to recharge them mentally or emotionally for another round of selling. They tend to use their break time as a distraction, a chance to check out for a while. Herbivores still feel sluggish afterwards, and by the end of their workday or shift, they feel exhausted and can't wait to go home.

Carnivores, in contrast, rarely feel that kind of exhaustion or burnout. They stay engaged, aware, and enthusiastic all day, even during breaks. The very act of hunting renews their energy rather than draining it—like a phone that constantly recharges itself without needing to be plugged in. Carnivores feel psyched up as they chase down their prey, no matter how long it takes. They know that if they want to stay strong and feed their families, failure is not an option.

This is why carnivores are able to end each day with my mantra of "Just one more door." You won't have the mental and emotional energy to knock on that final door or make that final call if you feel burned out. But you will if you avoid burnout by embracing the excitement of sales—the thrill of the hunt.

Of course, burnout isn't just a short-term risk on any given day; it's also a long-term problem for a lot of salespeople. I often hear pleas for help that sound something like this:

"I've been doing this for three years and I don't know how much longer I can keep going."

"My wife hates the fact that I have to grind so hard."

"I go home emotionally exhausted every night."

"I need to find a job that's more normal and stable."

Someone who talks like this actually has a mindset problem, not a burnout problem. I prefer to think of burnout as a physical ailment, like a coal miner or bricklayer who can't do their job anymore, because decades of hard labor have damaged their body. Is your body literally decaying? Have you lost the arm strength to knock on doors or get prospects on the phone? If the answer is no, you're *not* suffering from burnout. And that's good news! I don't know how to help a sixty-year-old bricklayer with a bad back, but I do know how to help you fix your mindset problem.

Imagine that it's the end of your sales shift and you feel mentally exhausted and drained. Then one of your best friends calls to share some great news—maybe they just got engaged or hit the lottery. I guarantee that you will instantly have enough mental and emotional energy to take that call and get all the details. Where did that new burst of energy come from? It's already inside you, but your friend's call brought it out in a way that your sales calls haven't been bringing it out.

When you get on a roll, selling is energizing. But if it stops being energizing, it usually means one of three possible problems: you're jaded, you're bored, or you're lost. You have to narrow down the cause of your alleged burnout before you can restore your focus and drive.

If you've become jaded, something about your gig is probably feeling unfair, and you think someone is screwing you over. Maybe your manager took credit for a deal that you initiated and scooped a commission that should have gone to you. That definitely sucks, and you have every right to feel angry! Try to fix that situation, if there's any way to file an appeal.

But you can't let that kind of injustice make you feel jaded and demotivated. You have to shift to the abundance mindset instead of the victim mindset. Yes, your manager is a selfish jerk. Yes, he stole your commission. But there will be other deals, and you can find future gigs with better managers. If you can't fix this moment of injustice, you'll have to let it go—before your sense of grievance and victimhood wrecks your career.

If you're bored, that means something about your work has gotten too mundane. Maybe you feel like it's Groundhog Day: Get up, call the leads, repeat the usual script, close a few deals, get rejected by most of them, over and over and over. The process isn't challenging or fun anymore, and you're sick of talking about the product.

Instead of accepting this boredom and letting it demotivate you, you can find ways to make your job less boring. One trick I used was to ask a friend to give me three random words to try to sneak into my pitches, and then I'd record myself to see how many I could work in. So let's say he picked *penguin*, *battery*, and *sushi*. I'd knock a door and start my pitch with "Hey, how are you doing, sir? Honestly, it's been a long day for me and I'm almost out of battery on my phone. I've been walking around so much, I'm probably waddling like a penguin. Can't wait to grab some sushi with my girlfriend later. Anyway, I'm Sam from the Acme Alarm System Company. . . ." Is that a silly game? Sure. Is it making a hard pitch even harder? Sure. But it's fun to ramp up the challenge and still close sales!

Another way to avoid boredom is to keep challenging yourself with higher and higher benchmarks, like a weightlifter in training. If I'm bench-pressing 215 this week, I can push myself to do 225 next week, and 235 the week after. Staying at 215 forever would be boring, but progress is fun. The same applies to sales. If your benchmark is cold-calling fifty people a day, challenge yourself to call fifty-five this week, sixty next week. If your benchmark is selling ten cars a week, what if you resolve to hit fifteen? If you're a realtor who has never sold a house worth more than $400,000, what if you challenge yourself to keep going after bigger and bigger deals? In any of those scenarios, you're generating your own excitement and variety, and squashing boredom.

Finally, you might feel burned out because you feel lost, which means that you don't know why you're doing this anymore. You've lost sight of your mission and goals as a salesperson. Or maybe you've accomplished your original goals but haven't replaced them with new ones. Without a compelling goal for continued improvement, it can feel hard to get out of bed each morning, let alone stay focused all day until you make that one final pitch.

The solution to feeling lost is simple: revisit your goals frequently, ideally once a week or even every night. Too many people think an annual review of their goals is good enough, but that's wrong. Don't wait until you hit one benchmark to think about the next one. If you plan ahead and stack up your benchmarks in advance, the excitement of knowing what you'll accomplish next can boost your motivation and momentum. Write it all down so you can't subconsciously change your goals after you set them.

Above all, remember that what most people call burnout isn't really burnout. You just have to find the why so you can restore your drive.

PART TWO

Overall Strategy

14

Introduction to Overall Strategy

NOW THAT YOU UNDERSTAND the priorities for developing your mindset, it's time to get a little more practical about the nuts and bolts of selling. In this section we're going to tackle some important questions:

- How do you figure out your sales goals so you can judge your progress as you continue to hone your skills?
- Why are daily routines important, and how can you create routines at different times of the day that will maximize your effectiveness?
- How many hours do you really need to work per day, week, month, year?
- What are the four types of questions that form the foundation for just about every sales technique? How can you get better at all four?
- What are the four building blocks of sales that you should start constructing from the second you first open your mouth?
- What makes an exceptionally bad salesperson—the kind who drives a customer away even if they want to buy?
- What makes an exceptionally awesome salesperson—the kind that a customer wants to stay in touch with forever and refer to everyone they know?

Let's get into it.

15

What Are Your Sales Goals?

THIS MIGHT SOUND VERY OBVIOUS, but many salespeople never bother to ask themselves: *What are my goals? What am I really trying to accomplish? How do I get to wherever I want to be?*

The way to figure this out is to break down those big questions using some basic math. If you try to skip this math, it will be like floating on a life raft in the middle of the ocean, with no land in sight. Which way do you paddle? How hard and how long do you have to paddle to reach land? If you don't know, you won't be able to pace yourself, and you'll probably never make it.

It's not enough to say that you want to make as much money as possible. A vague goal like that won't help you to break down the numbers, and then you're probably going to flounder. So start with a target for your income this year. You can revise it later, but for now just pick a total income that would make you feel satisfied this year. Then grab a pencil. I promise that the math won't be too hard.

To simplify this example, let's say it's New Year's Day and you want to make $100,000 this year by selling Taggart Widgets. You make a $1,000 commission on each completed sale. So:

$100,000 income goal / $1,000 per sale = 100 completed sales

Now you have to figure out how to get to those one hundred sales—how many pitches to prospects, how many demonstrations, how many closed deals, and how many actually go through to completion. Most types of selling require a cancellation adjustment to account for customers who change their minds after closing. Let's say that historically for Taggart Widgets, a cancellation happens 10 percent of the time. So:

100 completed sales * 1.10 cancellation adjustment = 110 closes

You need to close one hundred and ten deals to generate one hundred commissions.

Next question: On average, how many prospects do you need to approach, and how many of those need to reach the demonstration stage, to close one sale? Let's say you've been tracking your results, and for every ten people you pitch, one of them agrees to see a demo; you have a ratio of ten pitches per demo. And for every ten demos you do, you close two deals; you have a ratio of five demos per close. So:

110 closes * 5 demos per close = 550 demos
550 demos * 10 pitches per close = 5,500 pitches

The next step is breaking down those 5,500 pitches into monthly, weekly, and daily goals. This requires another big question: How much do you want to work? One of the great things about commission sales is that you can usually control your own schedule—but that also means you're responsible for your own schedule.

Let's say you want to take a month for vacations, holidays, and sick days. That leaves eleven months this year. If you want to work four weeks a month, five days a week, that gives us:

$$\text{11 months * 4 weeks * 5 days = 220 days}$$

Someone else might make other choices, like choosing to work six days a week, fifty weeks a year. But let's say these are your choices. The final bit of math:

$$\text{5,500 pitches / 220 days = 25 pitches per day}$$

Underline that number, circle it, and put a star next to it. Can you really talk to twenty-five new prospects every working day? If yes, congratulations—you now have a plan to hit your $100,000 income target. If not, you need to go back and change some of the numbers on your worksheet. You can reduce your goal *or* increase your work-week *or* plan to take two weeks off instead of a month. Or some combination.

The numbers you choose are up to you, as long as you're being honest with yourself. It's not my place to tell you if your goal should be $75K or a million bucks, or if you should work ninety hours a week or thirty.

The great thing about doing this exercise is that you'll know exactly where you stand every day. If you pitch twenty-five prospects, no matter how those pitches go, you're on target. If you talk to more, you're ahead. If you fall below twenty-five, you're behind. The numbers won't lie to you. They won't tell you you're doing great when you're not.

By the way, my company developed an app called Xpand that will help you keep track of your numbers, to make self-accountability much easier. It automatically compares your targets with your actual sales results.*

If you have a bad day today, you can make it up tomorrow. If you

---

* See the back of the book or xpandapp.io for more info.

have a bad week, you can make it up next week. But every time you check your numbers, you will know if you're ahead or behind. You will find out if you need to get better at pitching, presenting, or closing. Try playing around with the numbers—for instance, what would change if you close one out of four demos instead of one out of five? The rest of this book will help you improve your closing ratio.

Of course this is a simplified example, because you might have variable commissions for different products, or you might not be able to work the same schedule every week. But regardless of whatever complications affect your situation, you can put in averages or guesstimates for key variables. You'll still have a pretty good sense of whether your goals are realistic. If not, you can take action with confidence.

I can't urge this more strongly: write it all out instead of doing the math in your head. You might not like the results, but you will be much better prepared for success after seeing them on paper, or on your phone or laptop.

16

Your Daily Routine

I'VE INTERVIEWED NEARLY 350 of the world's best salespeople for my podcast, and I'm always on the lookout for traits they share in common. One key thing I've noticed is that all outstanding salespeople are fanatical about their daily routines, especially at the start of each day. They optimize every aspect of their lives to get a jump on the morning, and they're impeccable about sticking to those routines.

Does this mean you have to be 100 percent perfect in following your own routine? Of course not. We all have a bad morning sometimes, maybe following a too-good night out. Don't beat yourself up if you sleep through your alarm once in a while. On the other hand, it's clear that there's a strong link between how disciplined you are at following a smart routine and how effective you will be all day.

I break routines into four categories: your morning, your sales day, your nighttime, and your personal time.

Your morning includes everything before your first pitch: what time you wake up, what you eat and drink, whether you get your blood pumping, and how you psych yourself up to start selling.

Are you exercising? Are you meditating? Are you listening to practical sales podcasts in the car, or motivational audiobooks, or just something frivolous? How do you organize your to-do list? Everyone's answers will be somewhat different, but the key is that everything you

WHEEL OF ROUTINES

do in the morning should be getting you focused and energized to start a kick-ass day.

Unless I'm traveling, I start my day at 6:00 a.m. with prayer, meditation, reading, breathwork, some affirmations, and a full workout. After a shower I check my planner over a light breakfast, so I'm up to speed on my goals and KPIs (key performance indicators) for the day. By eight I feel amazing—totally pumped and ready to take on the day.

The next key routine is your sales routine, which is really the subject of most of this book. This includes ways to maximize your actual time selling and minimize all the other obligations on your plate. You also need a system and scripts that you can constantly practice and refine to keep improving your results.

I consciously try to do every pitch with the same flow, every closing with the same flow, every referral request with the same flow. If you watched me do one hundred presentations to one hundred unique prospects, by the twentieth you'd be able to predict most of my jokes, transition lines, and bandwagon anecdotes. Repetition and consistency drive constant improvement.

Another routine that many people neglect is their nighttime: What do you do in between work and sleep? Your first priority is to let go of anything bad that happened today, because tomorrow is a new day. It's so easy to let a bad day become a heavy weight that you put into your backpack to keep lugging around the next day. You have to get that weight out of your backpack before it drags you down.

A good tactic at night is to recap whatever good things happened in your notes or journal. What three things went especially well today? Did you improvise during a tough situation? What did you get done that you really wanted to do? If you underperformed your goals, what's the biggest takeaway you learned from whatever didn't go well? What's in your power to do better tomorrow?

Remind yourself that tomorrow offers the blessing of a reset, a fresh start, a chance to improve. Then take a deep breath, exhale any anxiety, and get a good night's sleep.

The last routine you need to focus on is your personal life. We'll talk about this more at the end of this book, about how you need to see the big picture beyond your work and your financial success. You can't disassociate from your family, friends, relationships, hobbies, and all the other things that make life worth living.

People talk about work-life balance, but I prefer to seek harmony rather than balance. I visualize harmony as a wheel with six spokes: fitness, spirit, education and enlightenment, family and friends, emotions, and finances. When any of these spokes are damaged, the whole wheel won't roll smoothly. So you need to pay attention to all of them and block time to build routines to improve each of them.

I also try to connect with other people who care about the same priorities—those who will trade tips with me about ongoing education or fitness, for instance. Sometimes you might need expert help to find harmony, like a counselor or coach to help you manage your anxiety or process any trauma or emotional baggage. Those things can all be built into your weekly routines. The paradox is that all the nonwork equity you build up will ultimately make you better at your work.

Now that you know the importance of these four routines, I urge you to grab your notebook or a piece of paper and start drafting your own. Begin with just morning and night, the bookends of your day. Here's an example of what your morning might look like:

- 6:00 a.m.: Wake up and immediately say ten affirmations.
- 6:15 a.m.: Meditate or pray.
- 6:30 a.m.: Jog outside or on the treadmill, depending on the weather.
- 7:00 a.m.: Shower and dress.
- 7:30 a.m.: Eat breakfast while reviewing your game plan for the day.
- 8:00 a.m.: Leave for work, with a sales audiobook or podcast in the car.

And here's what a night routine might look like:

- 7:00 p.m.: Dinner with family, spouse, etc.
- 8:00 p.m.: Reply to emails and resolve as many loose ends as possible.
- 8:45 p.m.: Write the next day's game plan.
- 9:00 p.m.: Relax with spouse, stretch, watch TV, read a book, etc.
- 11:30 p.m.: Lights-out.

The exact details are less important than the process of writing down a routine and trying to stick with it, then revising it if you find that some elements don't work.

Lots of people get into commission sales because they want maximum flexibility with their time (see the chapter on 1099 vs W-2).

They want to be their own boss and have the freedom to take a day off or start late whenever they feel like it. That freedom feels great, but it only works if you stick to serious routines most days. If you can't set up a plan that drives the hours you need to reach your goals, you can get into big trouble.

If you really want to be your own boss for the long haul, you need to act like a boss and hold your "employee" accountable. This includes writing down your four routines and committing to them, unless you have good reasons to change them. Otherwise your alarm will go off every morning and you'll think, *Do I feel like getting up or not? Do I feel like hitting the treadmill or not?*

If you start every day by asking those kinds of questions—instead of *knowing* what your morning will look like—you will put yourself at a huge disadvantage.*

---

* Check out My Favorite Books at the back of the book for some cool books that go into more detail about setting up powerful routines.

17

Sales Is a Contact Sport

I LIKE TO SAY that sales is a contact sport; the more people you contact, the more sales you will close. This means there's really no substitute for putting in serious hours. That sounds obvious, but lots of salespeople think they can save time by honing their prospecting process with precision and doing fewer pitches. Instead of getting more sales in fewer hours, however, they often wind up frozen with analysis paralysis.

It seems to make sense to focus on high-quality leads, right? That's why many reps start thinking, *I don't want to waste my time, so I'll only talk to prospects who are pre-qualified or who match the ideal customer profile.* So they study customer data from past sales and find ways to rank prospects. Maybe this lead is a 10, this one is a 5, this one is a 2. Then they concentrate on only the top prospects.

But here's the problem: If you get too selective and only talk to prospects who you've ranked above a 7, let's say, you probably won't have enough to fill a whole day of selling. By trying to avoid wasting time on low-value prospects, you can end up wasting *more* time. That's going to get you into far more trouble than pitching some prospects you ranked 3 or 4 while getting into a productive rhythm of sell-sell-sell.

So yes, if you have enough information to rank your leads, rank them and start with the 10s and 9s. That's a no brainer. But then keep going, down to the 7s, 5s, 3s, and even the 1s, if you have time. I have faith in myself that I can sometimes turn a weak prospect into a closed sale. Even if I can't, I know that trying is a better use of my time than not trying. If I spend an hour talking to nobody, there is zero chance I'll get any results during that hour.

So your first priority is getting into good habits that will raise the total number of prospects you're reaching out to every day. Then and only then can you also try to raise the average quality of those prospects. You might have tools to develop higher quality prospects over time, but that won't matter much if you can't get into the rhythm of putting in enough hours. More salespeople suffer from a quantity problem than a quality problem.

You can't fake hours; you either did them or you didn't. Many people look for a shortcut to success that requires fewer hours. While there are ways to get better results from each contact—this book is full of them!—none of those strategies or tactics will let you off the hook from maximizing your hours. If you want to be more successful, spend more time talking to prospects. Period. It's simple, but it's not easy.

18

Where Are You Spending Your Hours?

LET'S SAY YOU USUALLY WORK a nine-hour day, and it feels like a grind all day. But how much of your time is actually spent pitching potential buyers?

A great way to find out is to track your time religiously for at least a week, to see what's really going on. Smartphone apps make this very simple; just start the timer when you start talking to a potential prospect, and turn it off when that interaction stops. Then restart for the next one.

Before you begin this exercise, try to guess how much time you spend per week on these eight categories of time use. Write down your guesses so you can later compare them to reality.

- Finding potential prospects. This includes combing through lists, creating leads, doing funnels, or knocking on doors in a neighborhood.
- Doing pre-meetings or pre-calls to schedule presentations.
- Traveling between appointments, whether on foot or by car.
- Following up with prospects you already pitched, via calls, texts, or emails.
- Submitting paperwork, data entry, and CRM updates. This is boring but essential.

- Social media breaks. The screen time for each app on your phone won't lie.
- Asking existing customers for referrals.

And last but not least . . .

- *Pitching qualified prospects.* I put this at the bottom so you won't overestimate it when writing down your guesses.

Then use your timer and take notes every day from start to finish. I bet you will be *very* surprised by the end of the week. For instance, here's what one telephone rep whom I coached recorded on a typical day.

He started work at 9:00, but after he dug through emails, planned out his prospecting list, and reviewed his talking points, he didn't make his first call until 10:15. Five minutes later he heard his first no. Then he saw a new email come in that looked important enough to open immediately. That email led to some other tasks. By 10:45, he was still only on his third pitch call. By 12:00, when everyone in his department was starting their lunch break, his timer said he had done just 29 minutes of actual selling, with zero successful closes. About one sixth of his morning had gone to selling, five sixths to other stuff.

This crappy morning made him feel discouraged, so he took an extra-long lunch, then wasted another half hour answering an "urgent" question for another rep. By 2:00 he felt like the day was rapidly slipping away, and couldn't get motivated. Seemingly in a blink it was 4:00, then 5:00, then time to go home at 6:00. When he added it all up, he had been physically at work for nine hours but barely spent two hours talking to prospects.

When most people do this exercise for a full week, they find that their estimates were way off base. A forty-hour workweek might turn out to be only ten hours of high-priority selling, twenty-five hours of low-priority driving, paperwork, and follow-ups, and five hours of time wasters like social media or shooting the bull with coworkers. Some reps have even worse results than that.

Doing this exercise can feel like a bucket of ice water dumped on your head. But don't get discouraged, because this is actually good news! Now that you know the problem, you can get motivated to start restructuring your days. Little by little, you can fill them with more high-priority activities. You can experiment with various efficiencies, such as doing some Zoom meetings to cut down your travel time. You can automate your follow-up process with technology. You can make a rule for yourself that you don't get to check Instagram until you make ten pitch calls, and then not again until you get to twenty. The possible tactics are endless.

Bottom line: Time is your most valuable resource, and you have to be *very* intentional about where it goes. You probably don't need to dramatically increase your hours, pushing yourself to exhaustion in the process. Instead, you can squeeze much more value from your existing hours, by eliminating all those time wasters and inefficiencies.

More often than you might assume, the highest-paid salespeople are *not* the ones who grind the longest, but those who are most efficient at maximizing their ratio of closes per hour. The more you understand where your time actually goes, the more inspired you will be to allocate it more wisely. And the more your results will improve.

19

The Four Types of Questions (and How to Ask Them)

IF YOU WANT TO SELL BETTER, you need to master the four major types of questions and how to use them at different stages of your sales pitch. I like the framework in the popular book *SPIN Selling* by Neil Rackham. He distinguishes between questions that move the sales process forward horizontally and those that go deep vertically. Both are important, so you need to get the balance right.

The first type is the *situation question*. Early in a pitch, this one is designed to find out what the prospect is currently doing with respect to whatever you're offering. Without this key information, you'd be shooting in the dark, and you might bore the prospect by talking about something irrelevant. For instance, "What are you currently doing to track your billing and accounts receivable?" This fact-finding will help you aim for appropriate targets.

The second type is the *problem question*. Now that you've learned your prospect's current situation, you need to know what problems (if any) they have with that setup. "Are you happy with your current billing system? What problems would you like to see improved?" Hopefully the prospect will now reveal their pain points, which your offering will solve. But if they have no pain points and think their current setup is perfect, you'll at least save time by finding out quickly.

The next step is asking an *implication question*. Now that you've brought the prospect's problems to the surface, you need to know the impact or consequences of those problems. "If your billing and reminders system is failing to get some of your accounts receivable paid, how much is that costing you each month? What does that lost revenue add up to in a year? And how is that impacting your overall business?" The answers to these questions will ramp up your prospect's hunger for a solution.

Finally, you can then ask a *needs-payoff question*, which helps clarify the value of your solution. If you frame this question well, the prospect will draw their own conclusion about how much value they'd gain by going with you. "Imagine that you switched to my company's billing system, and your accounts receivable became fully automated and nearly 100 percent got paid. How much would that be worth to you?" You want to engage their imagination so they can envision what an alternative future looks like—not just in dollars but in peace of mind, reduced stress, or other benefits. Starting a question with *imagine* helps unlock their ability to see this future.

When selling alarm systems, I'd go through this sequence of question types to find out the *situation* (what the prospect was currently using for home security), the *problem* (a vulnerable house and security risk to their family), and the *implication* (a potentially devastating loss of property, or an unthinkable attack). Then I'd use some *needs-payoff* questions to drive home the conclusion.

"If you got our system, how often would you use it? Every day? Can you imagine integrating this into your daily routine, when you leave the house and when you go to bed? Can you imagine checking that everything was okay from your phone, whether you're a mile away or across the country? How would that make you feel?" If you get this kind of question sequence right, your prospect will virtually sell themselves with their answers, and you can proceed straight to the closing.

Now that you know the kinds of questions you need to ask, let's talk about how to ask them—and how not to.

First, *don't be a robot*. You might pre-map great questions for all four types, but it won't work if you pull out a list and robotically go through them. You don't want the prospect to feel like they're answering a checklist at the doctor's office. "How much do you smoke? How much do you drink? How often do you exercise?" That's an interrogation, not a conversation. You'll get one-word answers at best, if they don't shut you down completely.

It also sounds fake and robotic if you say, "Great!" in response to every answer. People know that not everything they say is great! If your vibe is "just tell me more and more personal info," they're probably going to put up a defensive wall.

Instead, you want your questions to come across as if you actually care about the answers, not like you're reading a script and going through the motions. Use your tone and body language (which we'll cover in the nonverbal section of the book) to convey that you sincerely want authentic answers. Try to ask every question in a conversational way that builds rapport. The more rapport you build, the more comfortable the customer will feel, and the easier it will be to go deeper into real answers.

The second principle is *go from broad to specific*. Broad questions are less personal and therefore less likely to put a prospect on the defensive. For instance, "How long have you lived here?" is a broad question and not too personal. Most people will treat that like small talk and answer it to anyone, even a random stranger. But suppose I'm selling alarm systems and one of my first questions is "Which spots in your house do you think are most vulnerable to a burglar?" That's way too specific and personal, until we establish rapport and trust. Would you tell a stranger that you usually leave your back door unlocked?

The third key principle is to *ask good follow-up questions*. Plowing ahead with your list of questions instead of responding to each answer sounds rude. Instead, you can follow up with something like

What does that mean? . . . Do you have an example of that? . . . Can you tell me more about it?

Suppose one of your questions is "What did you like the most about the alarm system I just showed you?" If your prospect replies, "The cameras," don't move on! Ask what it was about the cameras that impressed them. "Well, my girls get home two hours before I get home from work, and I want to make sure they're safe at home without having to nag them." This response opens the door to even more bonding questions. "Has that been a concern for you in the past, if they didn't come home when you expected?" Now you're into a pretty deep conversation with this prospect about a serious issue for her family.

A good salesperson pre-maps their four types of questions rather than trying to wing it. But at the same time, they trust their instincts when following up, to keep the conversation going. Blending those two skills is critical to building the kind of rapport that leads naturally to a close.

20
The Four Building Blocks of Selling

LET'S TALK ABOUT the four building blocks that most strongly influence customers and drive sales toward a closing. I call them *building value, building trust, building rapport, and building urgency*. What they have in common is that you need to start working on them from the second you first open your mouth.

FOUR BUILDING BLOCKS OF SALES

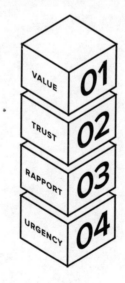

Building Value

Many reps do their best pitch with lots of enthusiasm, only for the prospect to say something like "I need to think about it" or "I need to shop around" or "I can't afford it." As you'll see in future chapters, there are ways to deal with those objections. But it's better if you can prevent objections by building enough value during your pitch and presentation.

You want your prospects to be not just interested but *salivating*. You want them asking themselves not, "Do I want this?" but "How fast can I get this?"

If you build enough value, you won't have to haggle over pricing. You won't have to counter their instinct to put off a decision. They're going to think, *I want this, I want it bad, and I want it now.*

One strategy is to play up different kinds of value for different kinds of customers. First you can use fact-finding and discovery questions to figure out what this person values highly in their ideal product or service. Then you can zero in on those criteria, recognizing that a benefit one customer cares deeply about might be irrelevant to another.

For instance, suppose you're selling solar. One prospect might care a lot that adding solar panels is super green and great for the planet. Meanwhile, the guy who owns the house next door doesn't care at all about the environment, but he cares a ton about slashing his electric bill. You can't use a one-size-fits-all approach to building value.

Building Trust

Trust is the most powerful force for overcoming resistance. You create it through the accumulation of everything you say and do—

including your tone, your expertise, your empathy, and your ability to listen.

Above all, you build trust by acting like a human, not a robot. No one wants to do business with a robot, which is why I'm skeptical that AI will ever improve enough to replace salespeople. If a customer is spending a meaningful amount of money on something (however they define "meaningful"), they want to give that money to someone they trust not to waste it. Someone they believe will deliver truly great value in return.

You want to come across as reassuring and low pressure. For instance, you might say, "I just want to make sure that we take this at your pace. I want you to know that I'm here to serve you and answer all your questions, to make sure you get outstanding bang for your buck. I'm happy to go down any rabbit holes if you want to."

If you succeed in building trust and projecting both expertise and sincere concern, you've taken a huge step toward closing.

Building Rapport

Please note that rapport is different from trust, even though a lot of salespeople get those words confused. Trust is about respect—do customers respect you as an expert in your field, and as a professional who isn't trying to rip them off? Rapport is about likability, which is also very helpful—unless it's all you have going for you.

Suppose you do a full pitch and presentation, and the prospect loves you. They're laughing at your jokes. You're chatting about mutual interests and other points of connection. You start feeling almost like personal friends. But none of that necessarily means they trust you. A lot of salespeople get frustrated when they build great rapport but not enough value or trust.

As we'll cover later, I call this *getting stuck in the friend zone.* You're having a great conversation about family and friends and their recent vacation and their favorite sports team. But all that rapport can't make up for not building enough credibility about whatever you're selling.

Again, likability is very helpful, and you should cultivate it as an essential skill. It's especially valuable when you're pitching extroverts who love to chat and won't get down to business unless they feel rapport with you. Just don't overdo it.

Building Urgency

The final building block, and maybe the trickiest to get right, is urgency. Yes, you want your prospects to feel compelled to buy quickly, not at some vague time in the future. But misconceptions about urgency—and an overdependence on urgency by many salespeople—give our entire profession a bad reputation.

Too many reps think they need to constantly ring the urgency alarm: *Do it today! Do it now! It's now or never! If you don't say yes immediately, you'll regret it forever!* Done the wrong way, which I'd estimate happens 80 percent of the time, calls for urgency only lead to mistrust, skepticism, and a reduction in your credibility. They can even lead prospects to conclude that they never want to do business with your company, not merely with you personally.

Today's more savvy consumers and business leaders know that they always have options. They can compare offerings from your competitors on Google. They can research alternative solutions. They know they can make a decision whenever they want. So you don't want to hit them with a sledgehammer, but you do want to gently shake that sense that they can buy some other time, no rush.

Very early on, you might say something like "Today what we're doing is . . ." Weaving in the word *today* is almost subliminal, to show that the two of you won't be dragging out this process.

You can also introduce external constraints that will force the prospect to move quickly. "I move around a lot and I'm only in your neighborhood today. . . ." That's not a hard sell, just stating a fact that shortens their potential time window.

And of course you can talk about short-term discounts, because we're all primed to respond to great deals on July Fourth, Labor Day weekend, Black Friday, and so on. If I see a killer deal on 55-inch TVs on Black Friday, I know I'd get laughed at if I tried to claim it five days later. You just need a credible reason why you're offering a special deal now that won't be available next month.

If you fail to build urgency, you run the risk of becoming what I call a *professional presenter*. That's a rep who does a great job educating prospects and answering their questions but is then unable to convert their interest to actual sales. You really don't want to go down that path.

AS WE GO THROUGH the next few sections of the book, think about how these four building blocks might be reinforced *throughout the entire sale*. You can start by writing down some lines you might add to your pitch and presentation to support all four.

If you try to build these blocks suddenly at the end, when you're trying to close, it won't work. You can't just say to yourself, "Oh, shoot, I forgot to build trust," and expect a good outcome.

Like a football team, you might call a Hail Mary in the final seconds of the fourth quarter, and it might even work sometimes. But that's a terrible strategy to count on. Instead, aim to put points on the board consistently, in every quarter.

21

What Makes a
Terrible Salesperson?

BEFORE WE MOVE ON from this section on overall strategy, I thought it might help to show you real-life examples of a truly terrible salesperson and (in the next chapter) a truly awesome salesperson.

I've never sold cars, but I know that selling cars is usually easier than knocking doors. Everyone who walks into a car dealership is a serious prospect, and they aren't going to yell at you for disturbing them when you start to pitch. They already have your product on their minds, unlike some homeowner who isn't thinking at all about solar or alarm systems until you show up. So if you get good at selling D2D, you can probably sell anything anywhere, including cars.

But just because selling cars is *easier* than D2D, that doesn't make it *easy*. I see many terrible salespeople at car dealerships, usually because they aren't reading the prospect and listening closely. They're mentally replaying a script or checklist they memorized, instead of responding with empathy to an actual human in front of them.

Not long ago I got interested in buying a Ford F-150 pickup, in red. An online search found only one dealer near me who had one. So I went there and a salesman approached. I told him what I wanted, and I even said, "Congrats, this will be the easiest sale you're going to close this whole month."

But then he started asking a bunch of questions that didn't matter to me at all, probably because that's what he was trained to do. The conversation went something like this:

What engine size do you want?

I don't know.

How many liters?

I don't know. I'm not an engine guy. I don't study engines.

What trim options?

I don't know.

Let me show you this white one.

Didn't you hear me say *red*? I don't want white.

Let me pop the hood and show you the engine.

Didn't you hear me? I don't give a freak about the engine.

Let me tell you about the gas mileage.

I don't worry about gas mileage.

Blah blah blah [more feature details] blah blah blah.

Hey, you're not listening. I told you I want a red F-150. You only have one red F-150 on the lot. I'd like to test-drive it.

Okay, sure, here are the keys. Go test-drive it and find me when you get back.

So I went out for a drive, solo, and found the guy when I got back.

What did you think?

I love it! It's badass! It's exactly what I hoped it would be.

Great, now let me show you a few that are even nicer.

At this point I lost my patience and stopped the guy in his tracks. I said something like "I'm not looking at any other trucks. And just out of principle, even though I love this one, I can't buy it from you. Because I coach salespeople for a living and, dude, I have to tell you, you suck at this! You haven't been listening at all since I got here. You couldn't even spend fifteen minutes test-driving it with me. What if I had questions on the road? What if I just wanted to share my excitement? So you're not getting a commission from me today. But at least you're getting some free coaching!"

I try not to be harsh with anyone, and I felt a little guilty for losing my temper and then walking out. But this guy needed some tough love. If he couldn't close this easy sale without pissing off a customer, how could he possibly survive at his job?

About a month later, the same car salesman texts me out of the blue. "Hi Sam, I finally figured out what you meant. I really do appreciate you. Let me know if you ever want to come back." I wondered if he had gotten in trouble over his terrible sales numbers. Maybe he finally realized he was overly scripted and sounding like a robot, instead of using empathy and intuition.

Memorizing key product details is important, but that's just part of the process. The sequence I teach is "memorize it, internalize it, then personalize it." I can deliver the same product information in many different ways, depending on who's in front of me and what the situation requires. The real art of sales isn't the memorizing—it's mostly *reading the situation*. If you can't get good at that, and if you keep talking when you should be listening, you can sell yourself right out of an easy deal.

22

What Makes an Awesome Salesperson?

IF THAT CAR SALESMAN in the last chapter was a cautionary tale, let's look at the opposite: a role model you can truly aspire to.

Perhaps the highest level of sales is when you build so much trust with customers that they stop thinking about you as a salesperson. You become their "guy"—their trusted adviser in your area of expertise. They tell their friends and acquaintances something like "You should talk to my insurance guy—he's amazing. Let me give you his number. I had no idea what I needed, but he walked me patiently through all the options. Then he made sure I didn't overpay for insurance I didn't need."

It might sound like a paradox, but if you want to rise to "guy" status (which applies to women too, of course), resist the urge to go for maximum value on every sale. To see why, let's look at the luxury car market. You might assume it's easier to sell high-end Mercedes and Porsches than Hyundais and Chevys, but it's actually just as hard if not harder. The challenges are simply different.

When I finally had enough money to buy a super-nice car, I got my heart set on a Ferrari. A friend referred me to his "car guy," Mike, so I made an appointment. The address turned out to be a private warehouse that housed the most amazing collection, like heaven for car enthusiasts. Ferraris, Bentleys, Porsches, Lamborghinis, and on and on. The cheapest one in the building cost $125,000, and the top end was over $1 million.

Mike was supercool and totally low pressure. After a few minutes of talking to me about what I wanted, he said something like "Sam, I could sell you a $300,000 or $500,000 Ferrari today, but I'm not going to do that. It wouldn't be in your best interest. You're making a big leap into the world of luxury sports cars. It's not like owning a normal car—you have to experience it to understand it. Every time you need an oil change, or some warning light goes on, or your tires start wearing down, you're going to have sticker shock at the cost of maintenance, and how long it takes. Taking care of these finicky cars is a learning curve, so you need to start in the right place."

Mike's pitch was already disarming my defenses as he continued to lay out a long-term vision. "Here's what I strongly recommend. Let's test-drive some amazing cars in the $150K range, and one of them will be your starter luxury car. Then in two years, you'll come back and move up a level, maybe to a Bentley. Eventually you'll be driving a half-million-dollar or million-dollar model. If you start out with too much car too soon, you'll probably have a bad experience, but you won't want to downgrade at that point. I'd hate to see the joy of owning these cars get ruined for you."

By then I was thinking, *This is the coolest sales experience I've ever had. I've never had a salesman even remotely as cool as you are.* By downselling me instead of upselling, Mike had completely won my trust. He wasn't really a car salesman—he was a *car guy.* He was thinking beyond one commission to a series of bigger future commissions. He told me as much while we were filling out the contract for my Ferrari.

"I don't see my job as selling cars. I'm here to build relationships with high-net-worth people—relationships that last ten, twenty, thirty years. Nobody keeps an exotic car for more than three years. I want to be sure you have a great experience today so you'll come back in two or three years and refer me to your friends in between."

Of course most products aren't like Ferraris. But no matter what you're selling, try to think and act like a "guy."

PART THREE

Nonverbal
Selling

23

Introduction to Nonverbal Selling

YOU'VE PROBABLY HEARD the rule of thumb that 80 percent of all human communication is nonverbal, and only 20 percent depends on the actual words you say. I don't know which researchers came up with those percentages, but they sound right from everything I've seen in sales and sales training.

Lots of people ask me for magic words, powerful sentences, and secret scripts that will lead to more sales. Although there's no magic language, there are lots of smarter ways to talk at every stage of the sales process. But honestly, none of my advice about words, sentences, or scripts will help if you suck at nonverbal communication.

You have to put some serious effort into *how* you say things. Start paying attention to your tone, energy, and speed when you talk. Invest some time and money in your appearance, which includes clothing, hair, posture, and body language. All of these details add up to how you'll show up for your customers, and whether you come across as knowledgeable, respectful, and likable.

Nonverbal communication goes a *huge* way toward getting any type of customer to give you their attention and give you a fair shot at selling them. Some salespeople absorb the importance of all these social cues in childhood; they develop nonverbal intuition on their own and don't need much coaching. Others need serious help just to reach a basic level of competence.

Wherever you land on that spectrum, I urge you not to skip this section of the book. I promise that if you take two salespeople with equal intelligence, equal work ethic, and the exact same scripts, the one with excellent nonverbal skills will close five times more business than one who struggles with posture, tone, and clothing. It really is that serious.

So as you read this section, take notes on what you need to work on. Then record yourself during pitches and play them back to see how you did. Or even better, have someone else join your sales calls and then give you blunt feedback on your performance, especially the nonverbal aspects.

It can be superhard to self-correct if you don't see yourself when you sell, and therefore you assume you're coming across way better than you actually are. That's true for every aspect of selling, but it's especially true for everything nonverbal.

24

Your Appearance

THIS ONE SOUNDS SIMPLE, but you might be amazed at how many salespeople fail at looking and smelling good before they approach a prospect. I'm not talking about reaching the high bar of a movie star or fashion model. I'm talking about the rock-bottom basics: avoiding bad breath, body odor, and sloppy, worn-out clothes.

The principle is simple: Nobody wants to buy from somebody who literally stinks or looks like they can't be bothered to wear decent clothes. If you show up looking like you just rolled out of bed, in clothes you've been wearing nonstop for a month, it signals a total lack of respect for your potential customers. Your appearance can kill your pitch in less than ten seconds, while they're initially sizing you up.

This includes your teeth, by the way. If you have bad teeth, please deal with that before literally any of your other problems. Go to the dentist or orthodontist and get adult braces. It will be annoying for a year or so, but then you can live the rest of your life with a nice set of teeth.

Maybe your parents taught you not to judge a book by its cover, but we're all freaking judges. It's just human nature! Male or female, if you're easy on the eyes—and nose!—it will be easier to get your foot in the door. Please note that this doesn't mean you're doomed if you don't look like Ryan Gosling or Margot Robbie. I've mentored and coached salespeople of all heights, weights, ages, races, ethnicities, and body types, and they can all succeed. The key is not the appearance you were born with, but how well you present whatever you were born with. Put some real effort into your grooming, your smell, your clothes, your shoes, your posture, even your nose hairs. Every detail counts.

Let's take haircuts, for example. You can succeed at sales with long hair or short hair or no hair at all. You can have a beard or mustache. The key question is, Does it look neat and professional? I used to have a ponytail and sometimes a scraggly beard, until my dad challenged me that I looked too messy. I protested that I was still doing pretty well. He replied, "But, Sam, how much better would you be doing if you looked serious and clean cut?" Touché. A haircut and shave really did help my numbers.

Of course the benchmark for your appearance will vary depending on what kind of sales you're doing. Some fields require a suit and tie (or the equivalent for women), in which case you need to buy those clothes, and go to a tailor to make sure they fit. An expensive suit won't help if it's too big, too small, or just wrong for your body type. Don't be afraid to ask for help at a nice store, or from a personal shopper or a friend who's good with clothes.

If you're doing some kind of sales that falls in between formal and "anything goes," remember that a little too nice is better than a little too sloppy. A good rule of thumb is to dress just one level above your prospects. So if most of your prospects are in jeans and sneakers, you should upgrade to business casual. Sweatpants would feel awkward with them, but so would a suit.

There are all sorts of websites and videos you can google for clothing and grooming tips. My main point is that you *must* think about this stuff every day before you leave for work, or even before you start your first video call. If you don't look professional and respectful, whatever that means for your situation, you're shooting yourself in the foot.

The other great benefit of putting effort into your appearance is what it does to your mindset. You'll immediately feel better and more confident in nice clothes. This is especially true if you also work out and get into good shape. Fit people naturally project more confidence.

25

Your Tone

TONE IS RIGHT UP THERE with appearance as a powerful, non-verbal way to get your prospects moving toward a close—or, if you get it wrong, to drive them away.

In my experience, three kinds of tone are useful for selling: *assertive*, *neutral*, and *inquisitive*. Be mindful of which one you're using at each moment, and don't leave it up to your subconscious instincts. Practice switching between all three in different scenarios, as appropriate.

The *assertive* tone sounds confident, firm, and bold, because you talk slowly and drop your voice at the end of each sentence. For an exaggerated version, imagine Batman talking slowly and in a super-low voice to some criminal. This sends a subliminal signal: *I know what I'm talking about and there's no point in challenging me. My facts are rock solid. My opinions are trustworthy. You should do this deal.*

You can usually save the assertive tone for the later stages of a sales pitch, as you're heading toward the close. It's especially helpful when responding to a prospect's hesitation or objections. Let's say they ask if the price you quoted is the best price you can possibly offer. Reply slowly while keeping your pitch low: "This is the final price. There's no way to go lower." Or if they ask for more time to think it over: "You need to make a decision now. You're going to love it." It's hard to resist Batman's confidence!

YOUR TONE

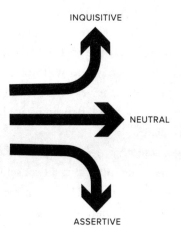

INQUISITIVE

NEUTRAL

ASSERTIVE

The *neutral* tone is also called the commentator tone, because it signals a just-the-facts way of communicating. At the end of each sentence, your pitch doesn't go up or down, it just stays steady. Imagine a classic TV anchorman like Walter Cronkite, or maybe Mr. Spock from *Star Trek*. The neutral tone's subliminal message is "I'm giving it to you straight, with no bias. Let me explain how this product works. I'm not being emotional, but you can trust me."

The neutral tone is good for the middle part of your pitch or presentation, because it encourages back-and-forth exchanges. It's not going to intimidate anyone into clamming up the way the assertive tone can. That's useful when you want a prospect to ask questions and get more interested and enthusiastic.

The *inquisitive* tone feels like you're constantly asking questions, even when you're just making statements. Every sentence ends with your pitch rising, which subliminally nudges the listener to respond. An extreme version used to be called "Valley Girl uptalk."

Use this one when you want the prospect to respond right away to what you're saying with their opinions and feedback. For instance, if you say, "A lot of people really like this. . . ." with rising intonation, you're not merely opening the door for a response; you're virtually forcing one. Same with a question like "Does that make sense?" which I often use to make sure the prospect is still with me.

As you practice these tones, you will notice moments in your pitch or presentation when they each can add value, and you can make notes in your sales scripts: "Be inquisitive here . . . be neutral here . . . be assertive here."

Then as you get smoother, your prospects may not even notice consciously when your tone shifts. But subconsciously, they will follow your lead when you want them to show interest and enthusiasm, or ask practical questions, or finally converge on a decision and let go of any objections.

26

Your Body Language

BODY LANGUAGE IS the sum total of all your physical movements, including how you're sitting, standing, positioning your arms, crossing your legs, gesturing with your hands, or making faces. Humans are hardwired to read body language to tell us if someone is anxious, disinterested, enthusiastic, bored, angry, and so on. We all read people subconsciously, which makes it *essential* that your body language aligns with your pitch. Pay close attention to what your body and face are saying, as well as what you can read from your prospect's body language.

It's a little hard to teach this stuff without video, but here are some key basic principles. If you practice these until they feel natural, you will signal that you're confident, relaxed, trustworthy, and friendly. It will seem like you've done this a thousand times, so your prospect can feel safe when listening to you and working with you.

- Try to match the other person's body language, to signal alignment. You want to get into a rhythm where you're both leaning in with interest. Gesture with your hands if the prospect does.

- Watch out for nervous fidgeting. There's a common scenario where a prospect opens the door and a salesperson starts tapping their foot while talking. The prospect will know you're nervous and

will wonder whether you're trying to scam them. Or they might think you don't really believe what you're saying about the product. Your nervous tics will make it very hard to get past this kind of suspicion.

- Hold your ground in response to aggressive body language. In D2D sales, an aggressive homeowner will sometimes answer the door with a glare and a squared-up, forward-leaning stance—the nonverbal equivalent of "get off my lawn!" When I was training D2D reps, I'd often see rookies lean backwards or step back in response. That reaction would show the homeowner that he had the upper hand because the rep was easily intimidated. I taught them to lean forward instead so the homeowner would subconsciously respect them for not backing down. You might need to fake it till you make it, in terms of your courage.

- Stand tall with your shoulders back. Slumping or slouching makes you look like a low-energy person who can't be trusted.

- Don't cross your arms. Standing with folded arms signals that you're closed off, defensive, and not listening. Open arms suggest that you're eager to hear what the other person is saying. I like to hold on to an iPad, clipboard, or notebook to keep my hands occupied.

- Similarly, don't hold your hands behind your back. It makes you look like you're hiding something.

ARMS CROSSED

HANDS BEHIND BACK

- Smile. Most people don't appreciate the incredible power of a simple smile to get others on your side, especially in a first-contact situation. Smiles are contagious and make whatever you're saying more believable. You can even hear a smile during a call! So if you do sales by phone, force yourself to smile while you talk.

- Maintain eye contact, but don't be overwhelming with it. It's a common but serious problem if a rep can't look a prospect in the eye. You might as well have a sticky note on your forehead that reads "I'm shady and not listening to you, so don't trust me!"

- On the other hand, don't hold eye contact so long that it starts to feel creepy. Break away periodically to point something out on your clipboard, or compliment something you see in their house, and so on. Aim for a good rhythm of a minute or so of eye contact, then glance away, then repeat.

- Nod your head to give and receive affirmation. If you nod and smile while saying something affirming like "This makes sense, right?" your prospect will be primed to agree. A head nod is so hypnotizing that you can trick a friend by smiling and nodding when you say something crazy like "You love eating dog poop, right?" They might reply, "Yeah," before their brain has time to process the question.

- Try the occasional high five or fist bump. They can be surprisingly effective when you make a point that the prospect agrees with. A quick high five or fist bump elevates the energy of your interaction, gets the other person more engaged, and uses the power of physical touch to create more trust and rapport.

- Lean in while the other person is talking, to show that you're listening, engaged, and enthusiastic. You can also turn your head a little and bring your ear a bit closer, to make this nonverbal signal even stronger.

- Take notes while they're talking, even if you don't actually need the notes. It's another simple way to signal that you respect them and are really listening.

- Another good position is shoulder to shoulder, which signals that you are sharing the same goal and on the same team.

SHOULDER TO SHOULDER

- Don't try to close while standing up, if you can avoid it. Ask to move to sitting at a table (kitchen or living room) for the final stage of discussing details and reaching a decision. This will make prospects feel a lot more comfortable and willing to say yes. Your prospect may resist your attempt to move to this friendlier, more open setting. But you should tactfully keep trying to get into a physical position where the odds of a successful close will go up.

- When you get invited to sit down for a presentation, try to sit next to the prospect instead of across from them, to signal a partnership rather than a confrontation. This applies equally to a kitchen table, living room, or business conference room. At a kitchen table, try to sit at two seats that make a 90-degree angle. In a living room, try to have one of you in an armchair, the others at the closest end of the sofa. In an office, take neighboring seats at the desk or table, or at a 90-degree angle.

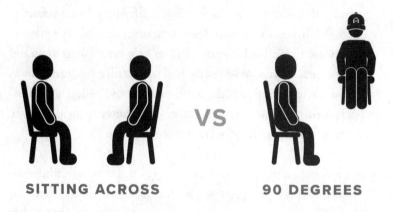

SITTING ACROSS   **90 DEGREES**

- It also works to sit side by side on the sofa, or in between a couple so they can both see what's on your clipboard or laptop. But make sure you don't sit too far apart.

SITTING TOO FAR

- Breathe deeply from your diaphragm to calm your nerves. Shallow breathing creates or worsens anxiety, and anxiety can be contagious. Practice taking calm, deep breaths, into and out of your diaphragm, to spread calmness and tranquility to your prospect.

- Pause to get the other person talking, then reinforce their responses. The more your prospect talks, the more engaged they will be and the more likely to buy. During a really great pitch, your talk-to-listen ratio may be close to fifty-fifty. Insert pauses to signal: "This is a safe place for you to open up and say whatever you want to say. I'm listening." Pauses help keep things loose and lubricated, because most people will talk to fill a potentially awkward silence. Then you can thank them or say, "Good question!" or another encouraging comment. Take notes on what they're saying to reinforce how intently you are listening.

I urge you to practice these tactics to bring calm, relaxed enthusiasm to your body language. I promise you that the effort will translate into stronger pitches, more responsive prospects, smoother closes, and higher overall performance.

PART FOUR

Prospecting

27

Introduction to Prospecting

PROSPECTING SIMPLY MEANS going out and finding qualified potential buyers for whatever you're selling so you can pitch them. You can think of it as the preliminary step before you get into pitching, presenting, and closing. Prospecting is the top of the funnel that will eventually lead you to closing deals. That makes learning how to prospect well incredibly important, even if it's not as sexy as closing.

The material in this section goes to the heart of the *eat what you kill* mindset. You need to think like a hunter, not a child waiting for someone else to feed you. *You are in control of finding your own prospects!* We'll talk about some creative ways to search for them, prioritize them, and make your initial contact with them. But none of those practical skills will matter if you can't get into a strong mindset about prospecting.

Too many salespeople never get good at prospecting because they get in their own way. They're afraid to take the necessary steps, or in some cases are too lazy. Or they pick up an entitlement mindset, thinking that someone else is responsible for prospecting while they can focus on pitching and closing. But remember: sales is a contact sport. Get pumped, get competitive, and get out there to hustle for prospects!

Of course, it's not just about the quantity of people you prospect—

it's also the quality. Planting your seeds in the wrong kind of soil is a fatal waste of your time.

So this section will help you improve both the quantity and quality of your prospecting. It's about learning how to put yourself consistently in front of high-potential opportunities, while spotting the duds quickly enough that they won't waste your precious hours of selling time. It will also show you why trying to cherry-pick only the highest quality leads, but with less hustle every day, is a losing strategy.

I've adapted some of the strategies and tactics in this section from some of my favorite sales experts, including Tony Alessandra (who wrote *The Platinum Rule*) and Charles Clarke III (who wrote *Bulls, Owls, Lambs and Tigers: Personality Selling*). Both recognized that you can't sell to every personality type the same way, so you need to be able to do a very quick personality profile of everyone you meet. My way of thinking about these four types of customers is the Driver, the Analyzer, the Passive, and the Socializer.

The Driver is highly assertive, focuses on logic rather than emotion, and wants to control the conversation.

The Analyzer is less assertive than the Driver, but even more about data and research, with an engineer-type brain.

The Passive is the most amiable, easygoing profile, putting personal relationships ahead of facts and figures.

The Socializer is the most enthusiastic and expressive kind of customer, combining the high assertiveness of the Driver with the emotionally driven orientation of the Passive.

After you learn more about each profile, you'll be able to quickly size up each type and know how they prefer to be sold. As Tony Alessandra put it, if the Golden Rule means treating people the way you want to be treated, the Platinum Rule is treating people the way *they* want to be treated. For instance, if you're a highly expressive and outgoing Socializer and you meet a prospect who's an Analyzer, you need to shift gears—play down the friendly chitchat and play up the facts and figures.

Once you get good at this kind of prospecting, you will be well on your way to carnivore status.

28

Customer Profile: The Driver

ONE DAY I WALKED INTO a department store to buy a new sofa. I found one pretty quickly that seemed perfect (I'm not super picky) but it didn't have a price tag. So I grabbed the nearest salesperson and asked, "How much?" Instead of answering my question, she started asking me a bunch of her own questions, such as "Where would it go, living room or basement?" I humored her for a minute, but then I started getting impatient. "How much is this one?" I repeated. But I still didn't get an answer, just more questions about my price range and an offer to show me several other sofas.

I got so frustrated that I left, even though I had found something I wanted and could afford, whatever it cost. Talk about doing a terrible sales job! She actually wrecked an easy close by not reading the clues I was putting out. In the language of the four personality types from the last chapter, I was acting like a Driver: above average on assertiveness and below average on wanted social interaction.

Drivers like me love to make quick decisions. We pride ourselves on keeping cool under pressure, without letting our feelings interfere with our rationality. When we shop it's business first, socializing with salespeople a very distant second. We're forceful, confident, and competitive, and we enjoy taking risks.

A Driver craves facts and figures, not happy talk or made-up stories. We want you to get to the point, clearly explain what you're offering, and summarize why we should care. We tend to get impatient, and you might see us roll our eyes if you try to BS us. Before we take a risk, we want the pros and cons to make sense. Many Drivers have successful careers as entrepreneurs or executives, and big egos to match.

The key to selling to Drivers is to challenge them just enough to make them take you seriously, but not so much that you truly offend them. They will perk up at a line like "You're probably not a good fit for our program" or "You might not qualify for our program." That kind of challenge makes them want to prove that of course they qualify.

They also tend to respond well to being asked for help, because that reinforces their high status. They respect a line such as "If this isn't right for you, that's fine, but could you please point me toward any other people you know in this neighborhood?" They may want to show off how many friends they have, and the mere act of giving you new leads can make them your ally. Then, once they're in your corner, they're more disposed to trust you and buy from you.

A Driver's biggest fear, in any sales situation, is being taken advantage of. So you have to win their trust by delivering value in your pitch. Give them useful information without high pressure. Get to the point quickly to show that you respect their time. Try to signal with every word and gesture that if they go with you, they won't regret that decision. And if they decide not to go with you, you'll still respect them anyway.

The tricky part is that while you're doing all these things to show respect to a Driver, you can't come across as either too aggressive or too timid. If a Driver feels like another Driver is confronting them, their defenses will go on high alert. But if they think you're a timid mouse, they won't take you seriously. So you have to stand tall—be assertive and respectful at the same time. Signal that you have a backbone and you're not going to let the prospect walk all over you, even if that requires walking away. Paradoxically, showing a Driver that you're not desperate to close makes it more likely that you actually will close.

Here's another relevant story, from when I was the sales rep, not the customer.

One day when I was selling alarms, a customer answered the door with his German shepherd right next to him. I started my pitch and he said, "Let me stop you there, dude. Why would I need security? This guy is my security." I could tell right away that he was a Driver. Very buff, with a strong personality. "No one would dare come into my house without permission. This is Texas—I own guns! If anyone breaks in, I'll blow their heads off. And if I'm not here, my dog will rip them apart. So I don't need an alarm."

I thought for a second and said, "I understand you, sir. But how about if we try a little experiment. Close your door but don't lock it, then walk out to the middle of the street. Let's see if I could get past your dog if I was a burglar." He seemed amused by this request and agreed to let me try it. When he was pretty far into the street, I opened his front door, walked inside, and started petting his German shepherd for a while. *Good boy! Good boy!* Then I walked past the dog into the kitchen.

The Driver came back into the house and glared at me. I explained: "Dogs can smell confidence as well as fear. So by acting confident and friendly, I communicated that I wasn't a threat." (I was tempted to add, but didn't, *It's just like handling a Driver!*) "If I had brought a piece of meat with me, it would have been even easier. If you're not home and it's just this guy doing security, your house is gonna get robbed."

By now my prospect was showing less aggressive body language and seemed willing to listen, so I continued my pitch. He wound up buying an alarm system.

Granted, this stunt was risky because his dog might have seriously attacked me. (Please don't sue me if you try this and end up in the hospital!) But I had an intuition that I could handle the dog, and an intuition that my prospect would respect me for trying. I was willing to get killed just to prove a point!

With a Driver, sometimes you can break the ice by puffing out your chest and acting just as tough as the other guy. Assertive people respect other assertive people.

29

Customer Profile: The Analyzer

YOU'VE PROBABLY HEARD that men buy logically and women buy emotionally. That's actually a bogus stereotype—and it can get you into big trouble. If you ever want to get smacked down, try pitching a woman who buys with logic using lines such as "Oh my gosh, you are going to *love* this, the way it feels, the way it smells. . . . Oh my gosh, everyone is doing it!" Women are just as logical as men, and many of them fit the personality type of the Analyzer.

Like Drivers, Analyzers avoid making emotional decisions; they rely on facts, figures, and logic rather than gut instinct. Also like Drivers, they put business first, social interactions second.

But unlike Drivers, Analyzers don't need to project assertiveness or take control of every interaction. They're more restrained and cautious, with faith that their analytical powers will lead them to the right decision. They love clarity and order, but not displays of emotion. Picture the stereotypical engineer or accountant—someone who's great at analyzing various options, but who comes across as a bit stiff or aloof, at least when dealing with strangers.

An Analyzer's greatest fear is being wrong, which would hurt their self-image as a skilled evaluator of information. This fear leads them to slow down and take as much time as they need to analyze a buying opportunity, in contrast to quick-deciding Drivers.

The key to selling to Analyzers is giving them lots of details and a complete explanation, from A to Z. You need to show patience while they process all the information you're giving them about options, pricing, and so on, so avoid any high-pressure closing techniques. By giving them enough space to analyze to their heart's content, you can build a respectful, trusting relationship.

If you make the mistake of rushing Analyzers into a decision, you will destroy their trust. Unlike Drivers, they get no satisfaction from conflict or confrontation, or any situation they perceive as you versus them. Your goal is to create the vibe that you're on the same team in the quest for an optimal solution for their needs. So practice slowing down your speech and movements, and moderating your tone. And don't spend too much time giving examples of what other customers did, because Analyzers don't focus on stories; they focus on facts and figures.

These people can be hard to sell, but once you earn their trust and get them on your side, they make the best long-term customers. They become enthusiastic about products they like and will be generous in making referrals.

Here's a good example. One day I was pitching a prospect about solar panels and asked what he did for a living. He said he was a software engineer, so I asked what kind of software. Turns out he specialized in accounting software, because he had been an accountant before getting into tech.

I knew right away that this wasn't merely an Analyzer but a Super Analyzer. If software developers and accountants are both left-brained, this guy would be Mr. Spock times one hundred. It was a good thing I asked, because his appearance didn't give him away. He wasn't wearing pants pulled up to his chest or showing any other geek stereotypes. But I could see that his car was a boring minivan, and his living room furniture was basic and well worn. He clearly didn't spend money on anything without a logical reason, and he wasn't going to chase any shiny objects.

I started my pitch by stressing the numbers: "I have a sheet that spells out how much money you can save over twenty or thirty years. It factors in the time value of money on your loan to finance solar panels, and how much you'll save monthly compared with your current utility bills. It also factors in likely future increases in the cost of electricity."

But I didn't actually want him to look at my printed sheet. I wanted him to run the numbers himself so he'd be more likely to believe them. I said, "Hey, do you have your laptop handy? We could plug a few numbers into Excel so you can compare your options side by side. I'm curious if it will make sense to stick with your utility company. We can figure it out in less than fifteen minutes." This made me seem like a fellow Analyzer, in search of facts and logic—not just some salesman trying to close a deal with BS.

We sat down in front of his laptop, and I gave him some numbers to build his own spreadsheet, along with what he found on his utility bill. Then he looked up and said, "Wow, this can save me about fifty grand." I intentionally kept my mouth shut while he stared at his screen. Then he added, "How come everybody doesn't do this?"

I replied, "A lot of people just aren't smart enough to understand the numbers. That's why my favorite customers are accountants, and I get the best referrals from accountants." Once the numbers clicked in his mind, he basically closed himself.

I've found that Analyzers get a dopamine hit from discovering a smart deal, the way other people feel jazzed about great food or music or sports. They get almost giddy if they figure out a new way to save money; it validates their entire approach to life. That's why great accountants love their work. Conversely, they hate being pushed into buying anything that's a bad deal, no matter how small. If they think they got bamboozled by some sales guy, they take it as a personal failure.

If you can find a way to let Analyzers work out numbers for themselves, instead of just asking them to trust your numbers, you will be in great shape. With some practice, you can close a lot of them.

30

Customer Profile: The Passive

THE PASSIVE IS the most amiable of the four profiles, combining low assertiveness with a highly emotional style that puts relationships ahead of facts and figures. These folks are social first, business second. They might be your easiest customers to close, because they will respond to an emotion-driven pitch and engaging stories about other customers. They take comfort in knowing that whatever you're selling has already helped lots of other people. They crave stability, protection, and peace.

If they like you, Passives will sincerely want to know what you think of them and their needs. If they *really* like you, they might call you *honey* or *buddy* or some other term of endearment. Their biggest fear is conflict, so they want to be liked by everyone—even by salespeople who reach out to them at random. They crave external validation and the sense that they're part of a group that's moving in the right direction.

The key to selling to Passives is to invest the necessary time to build social rapport and trust. Before getting down to business, they want to see you as a new friend, not an adversary. Then they need lots of reassurance that they're doing the right thing. So make sure you use language that addresses their fear of taking too much risk and going out on a limb. You can try phrases such as *Everyone who buys this really appreciates it. . . . Lots of people in your town are al-*

ready on board. . . . We've helped a ton of business owners with this product. . . .

On the downside, Passives tend toward indecisiveness and may lack confidence in their own decisions. That's why they have the highest cancellation rates among the four profiles—they often second-guess themselves soon after they've agreed to buy and you leave (or hang up). If that happens, you can appeal to the new friendship you've just established: "Hey, you're not going to back out on me, are you? After we spent all that time going over your needs and how we can solve them?" A moderate amount of guilt-tripping can get a Passive back on track, whereas those tactics might ruin everything with a Driver or Analyzer.

Many Passives are what the D2D community calls "one-leggers"— they can't decide without their spouse. The classic case is a stay-at-home mom who's nervous about upsetting her husband, a Driver. These women try to get rid of sales reps by saying they can't talk without their husband. But in many cases it isn't true that they can't talk to you; that's just a convenient excuse.

You can't give up on one-leggers; you'd be letting too much business go without even trying. You need to find ways to talk to them right now, because trying to come back another time rarely works. This is part of the carnivore mindset: if you have a shot at your prey, take it now! Don't let it get away and plan to come back later, in the hope that your shot might still be possible. It probably won't be.

I once knocked on the house of a young stay-at-home mom, maybe thirty-five. I could see a barber-style chair in her kitchen, with a floor covering under it, and she explained that she ran an in-home salon as a side hustle. Then she said she couldn't consider an alarm system without her husband, so could I please come back in a couple of hours, when he'd be home.

I responded with a technique we'll cover later called *objection fence staking.* "If your husband comes home tonight and you tell him you got an alarm system, is he going to be angry with you? Or are you allowed to make your own decisions to protect your home and family?" This positioned her to defend her own ability to make decisions, and to defend her husband as the good guy that he was.

I continued my pitch, and we got all the way to signing a contract. But a signature doesn't always mean a deal, because people legally have three days to undo an agreement. If I left now, I could imagine her husband coming home and making her cancel. I also knew that in general, once any installation work starts, the odds that a deal will stick shoot up to around 95 percent. That's why, especially with a Passive, it's important to get approval to start drilling immediately—to put the first hole in the wall before the customer can change their mind.

While she was reviewing and signing the paperwork, I texted my technician to come over ASAP. Then I positioned it as, "Hey, great news, our installation guy happens to be in the neighborhood and can get here in like ten minutes. This means you won't have to wait a couple of weeks like most of our customers." This tactic plays to the psychology that anyone who buys anything wants it right away. No one likes waiting.

Then I had an idea to ease her nervousness about the installation. "How about if I get a haircut while we wait for the tech guy? I've been meaning to get one for a while. I'll give you fifty bucks if you can do it now." She agreed and had me sit in her salon chair, and told me to take my shirt off to avoid getting it covered in hair. When the tech guy arrived, we let him in and showed him where to install, and went back to the haircut.

Then, amazingly, her husband came home earlier than expected. He found a technician drilling holes in his walls and *a shirtless young dude sitting in his kitchen*, getting a haircut from his attractive wife. He looked shocked and barked something like "What's going on here? Who the hell are these guys?!" An obvious Driver. He pulled his wife into the bedroom so they could talk privately. I could hear them bickering.

When they came back out, I said, "Sir, I'm happy to explain why your wife just made a great decision on this alarm system. You're getting a great deal. My tech guy is nearly done with the installation. But if you really hate our program, I can have him rip everything out." I knew that we had the upper hand at that point. Who would want to have a new alarm system ripped out, leaving behind a bunch of holes?

The wife finished my haircut while I talked to the husband about the deal she had already signed. Then I put my shirt back on and paid her fifty dollars cash, as my tech guy was finishing up.

Just another typical day in sales!

31

Customer Profile: The Socializer

"SO LET ME TELL YOU about our company's vision...." the salesman starts. But the prospect isn't remotely interested. In fact, they almost seem to be falling asleep. That's because this person is a Socializer, and the rep is completely ignoring their needs.

Socializers can be the most fun personality type to pitch, because they're both highly assertive and highly emotional. You can feel the energy coming off them as soon as you start an interaction. They're outgoing, optimistic, enthusiastic, and *very* social. They have lots of ideas and love to talk, especially about themselves. They're not as detail oriented as Drivers or Analyzers. Unlike Passives, they're willing to make a decision quickly—but only *after* they decide that they like you.

You can usually spot Socializers by how eagerly they interact with you. "Hey, welcome. Come on in. Where are you from? How long have you been in this business?" If you try to skip past all that chit-chat to dive into your sales pitch, Socializers will hit the brakes. "Hey, man, slow down. First tell me more about yourself." In this sense they're the opposite of Drivers. Their biggest fear is not being liked, so they go out of their way to engage with you on a human level, not a transactional level.

The key to selling to them is to slow down and play along with their need for social interaction. Look for any point of connection that you can talk about. "Oh wow, what are those beautiful flowers in front of your house?" Or, "Hey, I've never seen a car like the one in your driveway—so cool! What is it?" Or, "Hey, is that Coltrane playing on your stereo? I'm a jazz fan too." The more you get them talking, the more they will feel like they want to buy from you. Sometimes I've gone on a tangent with a Socializer for a half hour or more, but it was totally worth it. They felt listened to, like we were now friends. And they *always* prefer to do business with friends.

They can also be exceptionally optimistic, which makes them view your product in the best possible light, without you needing to exaggerate any features. A lot of Socializers work in sales themselves, so they can sometimes basically sell themselves. They get a jolt of satisfaction from saying yes and making another salesperson feel awesome. If they really like you, they'll also give you great referrals and go to bat for you with their friends. And because they're so extroverted, they tend to have the biggest social circles of any customer type.

If you find yourself selling to a Socializer, put on a big smile and say to yourself (silently), *This is awesome! I'm happy to talk to this person!* Ramp up your energy level, because the Socializer will appreciate it and will mirror your energy right back to you. Fire up your best people skills, have a fun conversation, and then you'll have a good shot at closing them.

Here's a classic example from when I was selling D2D in rural Texas. There are a lot of Socializers across the south who really want to chat before getting down to business.

One day I met an older man who had an extra barn on his property, where he restored old cars for fun and profit. When I approached his house, he was walking over to his car barn, so he invited me to follow him. I saw a bunch of beat-up old cars, and my instinct was to ask him to tell me about them.

Asking a Socializer to explain their passion is like letting a little kid run loose in a candy store. He started describing each car in great detail—the model, the year, what was cool about the engine, and what he was doing to tinker with it. "This is a 1977 Bronco, and what was special that year was . . ." I just kept listening and nodding and asking a few questions to show interest. It took him about forty minutes to give me the full rundown on his cars, and in all that time he never even asked why I was there. He was so stoked to have an audience that I could have been anyone.

When he finally asked what brought me, I kept it very simple. "Sir, I sell alarm systems and I really think you need one to protect all these great cars. You just explained how valuable they are, and you're taking a big risk by leaving them unprotected. We could get both your house and your garage wired up in no time." Five minutes later he was on board and we were sitting down to go over the details.

Remember, Socializers may need a lot of time to build rapport. No matter how much time pressure you may feel to move on to the next prospect, you have to act like you have all the time in the world. If I had tried to interrupt this guy's car stories to start pitching my alarm system, I never would have closed him.

Sometimes you may find that you spent 80 percent of your time with a Socializer talking about nothing relevant, or just quietly listening. They may even look down at the contract, start to sign, and simply ask, "So what am I getting here?" That's a sign that you did a really good job!

32

Create a
Prospecting Strategy

NOW THAT YOU HAVE A FEEL for the four customer types, we can get into the nitty-gritty of prospecting. It can feel overwhelming to try to figure out where you should be knocking doors, or which lists of people you should call, in what order. But if you adopt a few key principles, your prospecting challenges will get a lot easier.

PRINCIPLE 1 **If you don't have a strategy, you'll waste a lot of time.**

Salespeople who pitch at random soon feel disorganized and scatter-brained. They spend too much time on mediocre leads and not enough time on high-quality leads. They leave a lot of loose ends hanging. If they manage a team, they create frustrations and make their reps more likely to quit. In short, they waste a ton of time and energy and drastically underperform their potential.

Think about it: If you spend 80 percent of your day targeting people who blow you off, that's really demoralizing. You can do much better with a smart strategy than by jumping around randomly, like popcorn in a frying pan.

Narrow your targets.

You may think that everyone is a potential customer. But whatever you're selling, you can identify the niche that defines your ideal client, then focus on people who get close to those attributes.

When I first started selling alarm systems, I would knock anywhere. Then I gradually started to figure out which neighborhoods did especially well. For instance, in Texas, oil towns were always promising, especially if they were smaller, with no more than twenty thousand people. The richer neighborhoods within those towns were even better. The more specific I got in my prospecting, the higher my closing ratio.

But keep in mind that narrowing your targets requires a lot more prep time than winging it with an attitude of "Drop me anywhere and I can sell anywhere. I can adapt my pitch to any setting." That sounds like a cool skill to brag about, but it's not. If you narrow your targets, you can hone the best possible versions of your pitch and presentation. You will get dialed into the tactics that work and get into a winning rhythm with the highest-potential prospects.

So ask yourself three key questions:

- Who is your ideal customer?
- Where are they located?
- How can you find more of them?

Then you won't have to waste time wondering whom you should pitch next, which will leave you more time and energy for actually pitching.

PRINCIPLE 3 **Consolidate to create efficiency.**

This one is especially important in door-to-door selling, because bouncing around to different neighborhoods can waste a huge part of your day in the car. A series of twenty-minute drives in between pitches will quickly add up. Instead, plan ahead to consolidate your best prospects for the day so you never have to drive more than five minutes between appointments or door knocks.

This also applies to cold-calling—try to consolidate your prospects by specific demographics or customer needs. It's easier to create repeatable results when you focus on a single niche of prospects and get into a good rhythm with that niche. Then you can move on to another niche after maximizing the first one. This is so much more effective than "spray-and-pray" cold-calling, where you never maximize your results with any given niche.

PRINCIPLE 4 Plan to repitch.

As you'll see later in the book, it might take seven noes to get to a yes. If you work your way through a target list or a neighborhood, you might get a lot of noncommittal maybes or nonresponses. You need an efficient plan to go back to them, possibly several times. If you don't, someone else might build on the groundwork you laid and close *your* prospect. To me that was the most frustrating experience in D2D sales—I'd pitch a noncommittal prospect, but by the time I got back to repitching them, they had already bought from one of my competitors.

Make a plan to do systematic repitching, on whatever time frame is appropriate for your kind of selling. Use texts and emails as follow-up tools, when possible. But never just generic emails—make them stand out with a selfie or video message to capture their attention. Then if some new guy shows up with a similar offering, your prospects are more likely to go back to you, because you've already given them so much personal attention.

Remember that people's minds can change from day to day.

Maybe when you showed up on Monday they were in a bad mood, but if you repitch on Wednesday they'll be in a happier, more receptive mood. Or maybe the prospect had private conversations with their spouse after you left, and the spouse is now ready to say yes (or at least willing to cave). You won't know unless you repitch.

My most memorable example of this happened with a grumpy old woman in Borger, Texas. When I knocked on her door, she gave me a really hard time and refused to listen to my pitch. Then three days later I was training a new rep in my area, and we went back to the same house because I'd forgotten to mark down that I had already talked to her. I immediately remembered her when she opened the door, so I braced myself for another tongue-lashing.

Nevertheless, I started my pitch again, and within a minute she said, "Jeez, the other day I had a really pushy, awful sales guy here. You two are so much nicer! Come on in!" The trainee and I ended up closing her.

Good leads are precious, wherever they come from. Don't waste them by failing to craft and execute a strategy to get the most out of them.

33

The Importance
of CRM Apps

WHEN I WAS A NEW VP OF SALES at a solar company, managing more than one hundred reps, I thought my sales force had an average closing rate of about 30 percent, and my personal closing rate was about 70 percent. Those were just my gut feelings, but they felt strong enough to use when budgeting our marketing spend and bragging about my awesome team.

But then we committed to inputting all our data and tracking our actions much more completely. I was shocked at how wrong I was! My actual closing rate was 38 percent and the entire sales force's was only 12 percent. Not surprisingly, this inspired us to change our strategies and reallocate our marketing budget. Without that key data, we would have been up the proverbial creek without a paddle. I probably would have gotten fired in less than a year.

Ever since, I've preached that it's *essential* to use a customer relationship management (CRM) app to track your prospects and customers. This will help you know whom you have and haven't called or knocked, and what happened, and whether you should follow up with them. There are several decent apps and platforms including HubSpot, Salesforce, Infusionsoft, and SalesRabbit. If you work for a company, they may already have one that they require.

But if you have a choice, let me suggest a new, free app that my company recently launched, called D2DCRM. After seeing so many people struggle with mediocre prospecting and CRM tools, we built our own customized CRM with all the features we wished the others would include. We're giving it away for free to help salespeople like you; check it out via a free demo.*

Some people still prefer pen and paper over a smartphone or iPad app, which isn't my style because apps make data analytics so much easier. But ultimately what's most important isn't the exact tool you use, but your commitment to *consistently* tracking your activity, your time, and your results. Every day, every sales call.

Some companies also use these apps to create healthy competition among their reps, by using all that data to show key metrics on shared dashboards. You might not like having other people see how well or poorly you're doing, but it creates a heck of an incentive to keep improving. You really don't want to look like a slacker in front of your peers. Don't think of those dashboards as extra pressure—think of them as a game you can play to win. Put your competitive instincts to work for you. Then enjoy the recognition when your metrics go up.

And let's be real—the only people who complain about having their numbers made public are those with justifiable embarrassment about their results. When you're proud of the effort you've put in and the results you've achieved, you *love* to have everyone see them. So I take complaints about public disclosure as a red flag for a potential low performer who will need to be pushed and micromanaged, and who probably has an attitude problem.

Another reason you should learn to love CRM is that inputting all this data isn't just a boring exercise to make your bosses happy and help the company. It can also help you personally, maybe by a lot. If you pay attention, you'll notice trends in how much you're actually accomplishing, and with which kinds of customers and situations.

---

* Visit thed2dcrm.com.

Then you can adapt your behavior to do more of whatever is working best.

For instance, if you never close any customers that you contact before 10:00 a.m. or after 4:00 p.m., maybe there's a hidden reason why you suck at those times of day. The data might help you figure out that reason and address it. Even if not, at least you can change your schedule to do your most important pitching during your peak hours.

So your CRM app is ultimately helping you more than it helps your company. It can literally put more money in your pocket.

34

The Seven Doors to Reach Customers

THERE ARE SEVEN DISTINCT WAYS to reach customers, whether you're selling to individuals (B2C) or businesses (B2B). You need to be familiar with all of them, even if you specialize in just one. Sometimes you might be able to supplement your main strategy with one of the others, especially when following up after an initial approach. Sometimes you'll want to use all of them. You can never be sure which door will work, even after other doors have failed.

Because my background is *door-to-door* selling and training D2D reps, I'm biased toward thinking that D2D is the most challenging type of selling. It's face-to-face, belly-to-belly, and physically draining as you walk from house to house, or from company to company. You get rejected right to your face, not through a phone or computer. D2D requires more tenacity, willpower, grit, and hustle than any other sales process. If you get good at it, you'll set yourself up for an amazing career, because your skills will always be in demand.

But even I recognize that the front door isn't the only way to reach customers, and sometimes it isn't even the best. The next big one is the *telephone*. You get a list of leads and start cold-calling. The advantage is that you can be sitting in an air-conditioned office instead of walking the hot streets of a remote neighborhood. The big disadvantage is that you can't see the prospect's facial expressions or body language, and they can't see yours. (You saw in the nonverbal section of the book how important those are.) You also have to be really careful to scrub your list to omit anyone on the National Do Not Call Registry.

Then you've got *texting*, which is an increasingly good option because fewer and fewer people now pick up calls from unknown numbers. Text messages have been found to have an open rate above 90 percent! Whether people respond or not is a different story, but in the last few years, we've seen more and more deals originating via text. Don't dismiss it as too informal; that's not really an issue anymore.

Next you've got *email*, which requires a smart email campaign sequence of delivering lots of value before you ask for the sale. We'll say more about that in the next chapter, on follow-ups.

You've still got old-fashioned *direct mail*, entering someone's home through their mailbox. This is nowhere near as effective as it was a few decades ago, but for some products and some customer demographics, it should still be considered as an option for your arsenal.

You've got targeted *social media ads*, entering through someone's smartphone. For some kinds of products and services, especially local businesses pursuing local customers, these can be a powerful way to generate leads.

You even have *ringless voicemail*—software that sends pre-recorded audio messages directly to voicemail inboxes, without the telephone ringing first. Again, this will work much better for some types of selling than for others.

That's a lot of options for reaching a prospect, and often you won't know in advance what's most likely to get someone to listen to your pitch. So the challenge is being strategic about choosing the right door, or the right sequence of doors, for your specific situation.

Sometimes you might want to try all seven doors, because as Grant Cardone often says, it might take seven noes to get to a yes. Maybe sending an email that gets ignored is just getting one of those noes out of the way. But even if that email gets ignored, it is still subconsciously affecting the prospect's awareness of your brand. Psychologists have found that people are much more inclined to trust something they've seen multiple times, compared with something they're seeing the first time—even if it's a perfect fit for their needs. If you look at it from that perspective, no exposure to your brand is truly wasted.

Now let's look at a key principle for using these seven doors in your follow-up process: *data is king*.

35

Following Up: Data Is King

AS YOU EXPERIMENT WITH USING the seven doors we just covered, and in what order, keep one principle in mind: "Data is king."

Let's say you discover a new lead at a trade show, or as a referral from another customer, or some other way. Wherever the lead comes from, immediately make sure you get this person fully entered into your CRM system. You'd be amazed at how many reps get a business card at a trade show, or scribble a name and number on a napkin over coffee, but forget to enter details into CRM while it's fresh in their minds. That's a totally wasted opportunity.

Now you can begin a follow-up sequence like this one, adapted to your own needs:

FOLLOW-UP SEQUENCE

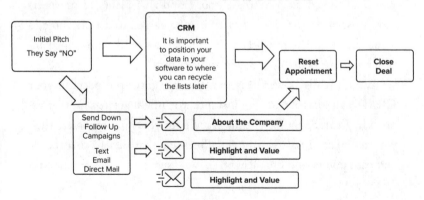

Let's say you make your initial pitch by phone and the prospect says no. Make notes on exactly how the exchange went. Maybe they didn't qualify. Maybe they're in a cash crunch right now. Maybe they already have a different software solution and won't be able to replace it for two years. Maybe they loved your product but their boss (or spouse) said absolutely not.

Whatever the situation, get all the details into your CRM, including the contact info for the person you spoke to, their manager, their territory, and any notes on timing.

Then you can experiment with a follow-up sequence using a combination of email, text, or direct mail. Personally, I prefer text because it's more friendly and casual. Just make sure you don't accidentally text anyone on an opt-out or Do Not Call list.

Your follow-up messaging should focus on adding value, not just hitting them up to buy over and over. Provide more useful information about your product or service and how it can help them. Gary Vaynerchuk calls this the "jab, jab, jab, right hook" strategy—you should aim to deliver value three times before asking for a sale again. Nobody wants to be bombarded via multiple channels if all you're saying is "Buy now! Buy now! Buy now!"

Craft your messages to be interesting, unique, and relevant to the prospect. Address frequently asked questions that they might not have had the confidence to ask you. I find that plenty of prospects have unspoken questions they feel embarrassed to ask. If you add value that way, the prospect will be much more likely to make another appointment and give you another shot.

What's really powerful is that you can filter prospects in your CRM by all sorts of data. For instance, you might create a list of prospects in greater Atlanta who manage IT for HVAC companies. Then you can create a narrowly targeted message that hits all their needs and pain points, and fire them off in rapid succession to everyone who fits that profile. That's the essence of data-based retargeting and re-marketing.

Data is king because the more data you capture and process, the better you can follow up. On the other hand, the less data you capture, the more you will just be spraying bullets with your eyes closed instead of taking carefully aimed shots.

36

Social Media Prospecting

A LOT OF NEW SALESPEOPLE naturally think they can use social media to ramp up their prospecting. They know a lot of people on LinkedIn, Facebook, Instagram, Snapchat, TikTok, and so on, and they see so much business content on all those platforms. If you search on YouTube for roofing, for instance, you'll find a zillion videos. Who knew that so many people want to watch people repairing and replacing roofs?

When I was at Vivint, the multibillion-dollar alarm systems company, I asked our marketing execs where we got the most and best leads. They said it was from our Snapchat ads, which really shocked me. I thought Snapchat was for teenagers, but apparently it's also for homeowners interested in alarm systems. So you might be surprised at how effective social media can be.

The challenge, however, is that you can't just throw content at these platforms. You have to create the *right kind* of content. That includes being mindful of whether you're promoting a company brand or your personal brand.

Putting company info on social media can be fairly straightforward. Everything has to be clear and accurate, featuring your product, customer testimonials, reviews by experts, and your company's statement of values. The main goal is managing your reputation and building trust—trying to stand out in a flashy way is more optional.

My company offers an app called Vanilla that helps small businesses manage reviews on Google, Facebook, Yelp, and so on.*

Today's customers are generally more savvy than those of the past. You have to assume they will research your company before booking an appointment or buying. They want to be reassured that your company has good online reviews and an appealing presence on social media. Anything you can do to improve that presence will give you a leg up, no matter how big or small your company is.

On the other hand, using social media on your personal platforms is trickier, because it's about your personal reputation as a human being in addition to your business reputation. A lot of salespeople tell me they don't want to put anything on their personal platforms because they don't want their friends and family to know what they're selling. My reply: if you don't want people who already know you to know that you sell something, you will never be highly effective at selling it.

Change your mindset by telling yourself, "I unapologetically want the whole world to know what I do, including my friends and family. Some of them will choose to engage with me. Others will refer someone they know to me. And if anyone disapproves, that's on them. I'm proud of my product and proud of what I do."

On personal platforms, don't use any kind of hard-sell messaging that screams, "BUY NOW!" You want to convey the excitement and satisfaction of what you're selling in a low-key way. Post to celebrate new deals and to say nice things about your customers. Then you can ask your customers to share those posts.

Let's say you sell Hondas. It's totally appropriate to post a picture of a customer with her new minivan, and caption it with something like "I just put Emily in this beautiful red Odyssey and got her a great deal. Wishing her and her family years of fun adventures in it!" Your

---

* See https://vanillamessage.com.

friends will like it, some of them will reach out, and some will refer you to someone else. As a prospecting opportunity, this is low-hanging fruit.

If your followers like the personality, warmth, and good vibes you inject into those posts, the scope of your organic reach might surprise you. People resonate with individuals far more than with impersonal companies, so they are more likely to share and engage with your personal content.

On the other hand, if old colleagues or high school friends stop following you, WHO FREAKING CARES? Let's be real—you don't really talk to them much anymore, and if they don't respect you for hustling, you're better off without them. The upside of using your social media platform to drive more income far outweighs any worry that people you haven't talked to in years will disapprove of your career. Your true friends will support you, or at least will quietly ignore any business content.

Another great way to use social media is via direct message outreach campaigns. Find Facebook groups, subreddits, and other spaces where your ideal customers congregate, and start to comment and engage with active posters. That will start to build more natural relationships with them. Then, when you start to DM such posters, do it on a high-volume basis.

Social media is just one piece of the prospecting puzzle, but it's an important piece and definitely worth your time.

Pitching

37

Introduction to Pitching

PITCHING IS THE KEY PHASE at the start of any sale—when you need to get permission to continue with a more detailed presentation, and then hopefully a closing. If you can't master an initial pitch that breaks the ice in the first thirty seconds, winning you permission to keep talking, you're not going to close many sales. You might try to specialize as a closer, but if you're not also a good pitcher, it won't matter how talented you are at closing.

I find that the initial pitch is much easier when you stick to a simple framework that looks like this:

PITCH FRAMEWORK

1. Intro

2. What

Problem

Program   Solution

3. Why

4. Pullback

5. Transition

The Intro is the super-important first stage of getting the prospect to hear the rest of your pitch. It includes building trust by quickly explaining who you are (both as a human and as the representative of a company), breaking their view of you as a potential threat, hooking their attention, qualifying them as a decision-maker, and enticing them to get on the bandwagon.

The What has three components: *the problem, the program*, and *the solution. Problem* is a powerful word, because it doesn't sound like a sales pitch—it sounds like a diagnosis. Then *program* and *solution* sound like an opportunity: "We're running a special program for people who have your problem, and you can be part of it if you qualify. This *program* will give you the *solution* to your *problem*."

The Why answers three distinct questions: why this program exists, why you're talking to this specific person about it, and why there's a special deal or discount available.

The Pullback is a strategy to create exclusivity, which is a powerful way to make people feel special and signal that you're not doing a hard sell. You actually start to take away the wonderful program you just introduced, because it's not right for everyone, and not everyone qualifies. You can't come off as needy! You want to seem almost indifferent, like it would be their loss rather than yours if they skip this opportunity.

Finally, *the Transition* gets you smoothly into the next phase of doing a demonstration, setting up an appointment for a presentation, or moving into a close.

How do I know this pitch framework works? I've personally seen it lead to higher conversion rates for all kinds of products, from solar panels to pest control to roofing to business coaching services. I even put it to the test a few years ago with *random* products that I didn't normally sell, knocking on doors for things like bounce houses and spyglasses. The framework passed every test I could throw at it. It's easy to customize for not just any kind of product, but also widely varying price points, customer demographics, and market saturation levels.

Now let's go through the elements of pitching in more detail, starting with the all-important mental shift you have to achieve within the first thirty seconds.

38

The First Thirty Seconds State Change

WITHIN THE FIRST THIRTY SECONDS of your pitch, it's essential to create what I call a *state change*, which takes the prospect from *I don't want to talk to you* to *I really want to keep talking to you*.

There are five types of emotions that can drive this state change—*connection*, *appreciation*, *authority*, *curiosity*, and *urgency*—and you can deploy all of them via your tone, words, body language, and overall energy.

These tactics apply whether you're selling to individuals or businesses. If you show up without an appointment, both homeowners and business owners are likely to use a quick excuse to get rid of you, such as "I'm too busy to talk" or "We don't allow solicitors in here." Things can get especially awkward if you walk into a store and the energy of the staff shifts from "Hey, here's a potential customer!" to "Oh crap, here's a salesperson." That's the moment when you need to dig deep, summon your courage, and go after the five emotions you need to bring out.

Connection is simply finding common ground as a fellow human being. Many people have been taught to see a salesperson as almost as bad as a pickpocket or con artist. They will treat you warily at best, like you're a dangerous zoo animal who might strike if they stick their hand inside the cage. During a D2D pitch, they might keep their storm door closed, so there's literally a glass wall between you. (Do they really think an unlocked storm door would stop an actual attacker? I'd love to ask a psychologist what's up with that.)

Your first job is to signal that you're not a zoo animal or any kind of attacker, just a normal person. Look for any point of connection to establish common ground: "Hey, I see Legos on the floor—how old are your kids? I have three under ten and my house has Legos everywhere!" Or: "I noticed the University of Utah sticker on your car—my dad went there and my uncle played football there. I love that school!" We'll get into more connection tactics in the next chapter, but the key is that personal questions need to feel like casual conversation, not a police interrogation. It can sound really creepy if you're too serious when you ask something like "Are you married? Do you have kids?" If you slip into a tone or body language that seems invasive, those questions might get the door slammed in your face.

In a perfect scenario, your point of personal connection will lead naturally into whatever you're selling. For instance, if you're selling alarm systems and learn that both you and the prospect have little kids, you can sincerely say how much you used to worry about protecting your family, until you got an excellent home security system.

Appreciation sounds obvious, yet many salespeople skip it. Just add something as simple as, "Thank you so much for taking the time to hear me out. There's a lot of mean people out there, and just the fact that you're willing to give me five minutes makes me so grateful. I hope that when I'm done, you'll agree that I didn't waste your time." People love appreciation, but you actually have to feel it, not just say it.

You can even use appreciation to frame the entire conversation, before the other person says anything. Try something like "All of your neighbors have been so receptive, it's amazing. You must love living here with all these nice people. Thanks for taking the time to hear me out." It's hard for any homeowner to act like a jerk at that point.

Authority is quickly conveying that you're an expert, you know what you're talking about, and you have some kind of credentials. For instance: "Hi, I'm in charge of the Weatherwatch program. You probably got the notice from the National Weather Service on January 13, and it's very important that everyone in town gets up to speed with the new mandate." Of course the prospect will want you to explain that mandate!

You can also show some kind of relevant printed-out article, license, or permit that signals authority. During a phone pitch you can refer to government agencies, like the Energy Department or the IRS, without actually claiming that you represent those agencies. Sometimes simply using more sophisticated words or phrases will do the trick, especially if you also use an authoritative tone.

Curiosity is about making prospects feel like they're not aware of something important. No one wants to feel like they're missing anything significant in their world. It can be as easy as throwing out a cryptic statement such as "I'm sure you know that a lot of people are concerned about what's been happening over on 30 East." *Wait, what? What's been going on on 30 East?* Now you've got them hooked until their curiosity is satisfied.

Finally, in the first thirty seconds you can begin to inject *urgency*. No one wants to miss an opportunity that can't be postponed. I still do most of my Christmas shopping on Black Friday, even though I hate it, because I hate to miss out on special deals. Most people are natural procrastinators, but a short-term deal or impending deadline is often enough to neutralize procrastination.

So you might say something like "Today's my last day meeting people in your neighborhood, but before I wrap up and leave town, I didn't want to leave you out. So if you can't talk now I'm sorry, but I won't be back." Or you can impose an artificial deadline: "This discounted program was supposed to expire October 31, but the state is giving us a grace period to qualify until November 13. So if you talk to me today, I can get you in right under the wire." Just be careful not to overdo it with overly aggressive deadlines, because they may sound fake and too salesy. You're looking for the sweet spot where the prospect feels an urgent need to listen to you, but doesn't think you're full of crap about a fake deadline.

It might seem like I'm asking you to squeeze a huge amount of content into thirty seconds to achieve the state change in the mind of your prospect. But these five elements can emerge naturally if you build them into your pitch opening. The key is preparation—mapping out what messages you need to convey right up front, and practicing them with variations. Write down some connection points, some appreciation phrases, some authority markers, some cryptic statements that provoke curiosity, and so on. Practice them over and over so you'll feel comfortable riffing on them and tweaking them to meet specific situations.

The tactics of your pitch opening will take all five of these emotional elements well beyond the first thirty seconds, as you'll see in the next chapter.

39

Step 1: The Opening

THE OPENING IS IN MANY WAYS the most important part of your pitch. As we saw in the last chapter, you should assume you have only thirty seconds to win enough attention and trust that you'll be allowed to keep going. The main goal of the opening is to buy yourself more time and solidify the state change you'll hopefully achieve in the first thirty seconds.

If you can't get good at opening, it won't matter how good you are at closing. I'm always amazed at how many people ask my company for closing training, when their biggest struggle is actually starting a pitch, engaging a prospect, and winning permission to keep the conversation going. Closing may be sexier than opening, but the initial hurdle of simply getting someone to listen to you, instead of hanging up or slamming the door, is truly make or break.

There are several powerful tactics to help you ace the opening.

I call the first one *breaking preoccupation*. Imagine there's a wall in between you and the prospect, and when you first show up, he's peeking at you over the top of that wall. He's suspicious or annoyed because he's preoccupied with something else and doesn't want to shift his attention. Your goal is to erase that wall as fast as possible and move into a position where you and the prospect are on the same side, both now focused on the same issue and looking at the world as teammates.

PITCH OPENING

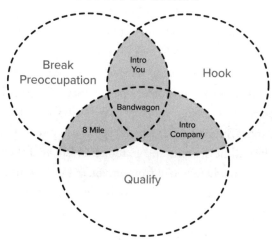

If you're selling in person, try to soften your body language, which the prospect might subconsciously mimic. On the phone especially, *use an easygoing, nonaggressive tone.* It helps if you can come up with *a simple, authentic joke* and test it to make sure it works every time. Then watch for signs that the prospect is dropping their guard and ready to have a real conversation. We're friends now!

Even better, *give an authentic compliment* about something you just noticed—their car, their necklace, the landscaping in front of their house. This can be harder on the phone, but maybe the prospect has an unusual first name that you can say something nice about.

I was always on the lookout for women who crocheted, because I learned to crochet in high school, when I was stuck in bed for months with a broken pelvis. Whenever I complimented someone's crocheted window tassels or tablecloth, it completely broke their expectations of what a young dude would notice and appreciate. I could even identify a shell stitch! It was the perfect icebreaker and bonding moment.

Another great way to not come across like a pushy salesperson is to *ask a random question* unrelated to your pitch. For instance: "I love this neighborhood—how long have you guys lived here?" Or: "Do you know Susan down the block? I was just talking to her, and she's a real hoot." This nudges the prospect's brain toward your question and away from their naturally defensive posture.

As you pivot to *introducing yourself*, you should have at least a preliminary sense of the customer's personality type (see the earlier chapters on the four major types). This will help you adjust your language and tone. But no matter which type you're pitching, you want to project friendliness. Smile and go for a handshake if they seem receptive. Mention where you're from, if you're local. It all reinforces the message that you're a fellow human being, even when you disclose that you represent a company offering something for sale.

Right after your introduction is a good time to begin *bandwagoning*, which shows that you've already worked with some other folks your prospect knows. Most find it reassuring to hear that their neighbors, colleagues, or other kinds of peers are already on board with whatever you're selling. Of course, this only works if you've actually closed some customers in their social circle. We'll talk more about bandwagoning in the chapter on the *Why* of your pitch.

A variation on bandwagoning is mentioning any famous or influential people who customers might respect. If you can honestly say that Shaq or Taylor Swift uses Product X, that will keep them listening for more details. Or you can name-drop an influential category of noncelebrities, such as "We set up a ton of doctors with our alarm systems." Of course doctors don't know any more about alarm systems than anyone else, but people assume that doctors are smart and do their homework. That will nudge the prospect to keep listening, which is all you want at this point.

The next key tactic is *a hook that generates curiosity*. This might come even before you introduce yourself and your company. You might lead with something like "Has anyone in the neighborhood told you what's going on?" That question is hard to ignore—what if something weird or dangerous is going on? Or, "Did Tiffany tell you I'd be calling? She was emailing everyone on your block about our new program." Anyone would be curious who Tiffany is and why they didn't get her email.

Or you can try a hook that projects *authority*: "Hi, this is my permit with the city. I'm in charge of this area. You're next on my list to talk to." *OMG, what is this about?* Whatever hook you choose (serious, funny, or just surprising), it has to keep people listening to find out who you are and why you're talking to them.

Then you throw in what I call *the 8-Mile tactic*, to overcome the most common objections before the prospect can even bring them up. ("It's too expensive . . . it will take too long" . . . and so on.) We'll explore this kind of "pre-buttal" later in the book, when we dive into objections and how to overcome them.

Finally, I believe that *qualifying the prospect* should be taken care of before you finish your opening. It's easy to spend a long time in conversation with someone who has no authority to make any decisions. Maybe they're just a guest in the house, or they live with their parents and Mom makes all the decisions. Or maybe they can't buy anything without having their spouse involved. Or maybe you've cold-called a small business and connected with someone who has no power to spend money. The sooner you qualify the prospect, the less time you'll waste in those situations.

I promise that if you practice interweaving these key tactics into your opening—some tried-and-true lines or jokes to break preoccupation, a pithy way to introduce yourself and your company, some hooks to draw curiosity, some bandwagoning facts, some 8-Mile pre-buttals, and some quick questions to qualify the prospect—you will consistently earn yourself another two minutes, and then another five.

Remember: You're *not* trying to close anyone at this point. You're just easing into the conversation and winning the right to continue.

40

Step 2: The What

NOW THAT YOU'RE PAST the opening phase of your pitch, you've achieved the state change, and the prospect is primed to listen, it's time to get into *the What*. I find that it's much easier to explain whatever you're offering if you think of it as three distinct components: *the problem*, *the program*, and *the solution*.

Problem is a powerful word, because it doesn't sound like a sales pitch—it sounds like a diagnosis. As soon as people understand that

THE "WHAT" CIRCLE

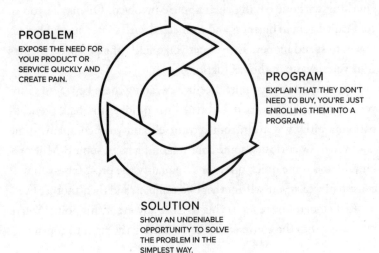

PROBLEM
EXPOSE THE NEED FOR YOUR PRODUCT OR SERVICE QUICKLY AND CREATE PAIN.

PROGRAM
EXPLAIN THAT THEY DON'T NEED TO BUY, YOU'RE JUST ENROLLING THEM INTO A PROGRAM.

SOLUTION
SHOW AN UNDENIABLE OPPORTUNITY TO SOLVE THE PROBLEM IN THE SIMPLEST WAY.

they have a problem, they crave a solution. That usually makes them willing to hear about your program.

Let's say you're selling D2D for a company that does roof replacements, which is a big project that homeowners don't jump into casually. The traditional roofing sales pitch stresses that homeowner's insurance will often cover a new roof. I've seen residential neighborhoods totally saturated with reps who all use the same approach: "We can get your insurance to pay for a new roof; you just have to pay the deductible." If you're the tenth rep making that pitch, you're so late to the party that you have no chance.

Instead, I would lead with the *problem* of how much damage an old roof can cause. "It might be fine now, but what happens when the next hurricane or heavy thunderstorm comes through? Do you want to wait until your living room and bedroom are badly flooded before dealing with that problem?"

Then I'd slide into the *program* that provides the *solution*: "My company is running a special new program we call No Roof Left Behind. We start with a free inspection of your roof to see how much it has deteriorated. If it's still in good condition, that would be great news for you. You'll have peace of mind without paying a dime. But if you do qualify for our new program, we can deal with all the hassles of the insurance claim. We'll file the claim and make sure you get approved before we start any work. I'm sure you're cautious about not getting stuck with a big bill. Don't worry, we know how to deal with all the insurance companies. All you'll have to pay is your small deductible."

Can you see the difference in impact when you frame the *What* around the problem first, instead of skipping directly to the features of your product or service? Now let's see how it works for a very different product, one not nearly as dramatic as a potentially flooded house.

I have a coaching client who sells candles as a subscription service, delivering a new batch every three months. (Apparently there are a lot of people who collect fancy scented candles—who knew?) The problem she solves for her customers is lack of consistency. The typical candle fan bounces from store to store, buying all sorts of candles in different sizes and shapes and scents. When the customer puts them on display, they all clash with each other. They look bad and maybe they smell funny, even when they aren't lit.

So my client offers a simple program to solve this problem. "We make sure you have a steady, affordable supply of candles that all go together. They look great, they smell great, and they're eco-friendly. They will bring comfort, peace, and tranquility into your home, and no one will think you just threw together a random bunch of candles. You can get as wide a variety as you like, and if you have a few scents you especially love, you can easily customize your delivery every three months. You will always have a fresh-smelling home, running on autopilot. And if you qualify for our limited-time program, I'll get you a 50 percent discount on your first two shipments."

Whatever you're selling, it's not really about the thing itself—it's about how the thing will help your customer. That message needs to be super clear and near the top of your pitch framework sequence.

41

Step 3: The Why

THE WHY PHASE OF your pitch can include three distinct kinds of why:

- Why this program exists
- Why you're talking to this specific person
- Why there's a special deal or discount available

Why This Program Exists

You can't just say, "Hey, here's this thing, do you want it?" Prospects need to know *why* you're calling them or at their door. Which boils down to two questions:

- What's in it for me?
- What's in it for you?

If there isn't a justification of why they should take more time to care, you will get rejected *super* fast.

An example from selling insurance: "I'm calling because the laws just changed in your state about health insurance options. Our company has found that if we help families understand the new updates, we can provide them with a cheaper way to get better coverage. Most tend to switch over to take advantage of this opportunity."

Or let's return to my friend with the candle subscription service. She needs a strong *Why* to counter the most common objection she hears from prospects: "I already have enough candles, and if I run out I can just go to the store. So why should I subscribe?"

Her *Why* response is "I know you love nice-smelling candles in your home. Our program exists because our customers don't want to have to even think about running out of candles. They set up with us, and then they can just enjoy their candles, with no hassles. If they ever want to change up the scents, or add more or fewer candles to their regular order, that's easy too—just a few clicks online or a quick call. And unlike shopping in stores, you'll know that our quality is consistently good, and you're getting a 20 percent discount off the list price."

Why You're Talking to This Specific Person

Here's where you can expand the bandwagoning that you may have begun during your opening. The power of bandwagoning is that no one wants to be the first in their neighborhood or social circle to buy something. If you can confirm that others have already validated your company, the quality of your product, and the value of your program, skepticism will drop dramatically.

My favorite tactic for bandwagoning is the name list. During a D2D pitch, I'll take out a list of other customers in the area and ask who the prospect might know. Let's say they reply, "I know John, he's the principal of my kid's school. Sarah lives around the corner and I see her sometimes." Please note that folks on your name list don't have to be the prospect's close friends. Just normal people in town, to prove that buying from you isn't crazy. The list instantly generates trust—not 100 percent trust, but enough to win you permission to keep talking.

Then I'll say something like "John and Sarah both got great deals on our security program. You know Sarah has two kids in high school and one in middle school, right? She told me her high school junior kept sneaking out at night. Now Sarah gets a notification on her phone every time a door or window opens, so she knows what's going on. She can sleep soundly again."

Your goal is to share the details of at least one "doppelgänger" customer who was in a similar situation as your prospect. In this example, maybe the person you're pitching thinks her kids are perfect angels and would never sneak out at night, but you can say that every parent thinks that's true, including Sarah! So the reason you're at her door is that you know she would gain peace of mind from your program, just like her neighbor did.

You can also do group profiling, such as stressing that lots of doctors buy your alarm system. If you're selling insurance, you can stress that a lot of attorneys and small business owners buy a particular insurance program, when pitching folks in those demographics.

I once pitched a business owner who tried to shut me down right away, saying he'd had the same insurance salesman for twenty years and wasn't looking for anything new. I said, "That's what the owners of Lux Auto, Prime Corporate, Elite Mortgage, and Perry's Collision also told me. But they were all super surprised when I gave them a simple breakdown of the numbers, and they went with me. I'm just asking if you can hear me out for thirty seconds. Then if you don't like it, I'll get out of your hair." Mentioning those doppelgänger customers got me the attention I needed to make my pitch, and he ended up loving it.

Bandwagoning makes your prospects feel like you've chosen them for a good reason, that you aren't just pitching anyone and everyone.

It builds credibility and trust. It breaks through common objections. And it focuses the listener on specific features and benefits that will appeal to them.

Why There's a Special Deal or Discount Available

The third kind of why heads off the understandable suspicion that if you're offering a great deal, there must be a catch. Promising customers too much generosity is a red flag.

You can solve this by explaining a win-win scenario that shows how your company and the customer will both benefit. For example, for that candle subscription service: "The value of this program for us is that we can predict how many candles we'll need each month for all our customers. So we get better deals from our suppliers, and then we pass along a lot of that savings to you. Everyone benefits."

Another example, for alarm systems: "If you qualify for this special program, we'll waive your installation fee, your activation fee, and your first-year warranty fee. Now you might be wondering why we'd be that generous. It's because if you like the service, we're going to ask you for the names of a few neighbors who might also like it, so we can tell them you're a satisfied customer. And we're going to ask you to put a little sign with our company name in your front yard. That seems like a fair give-and-take, right? Are you cool with that?"

Another good example is a company that cuts its marketing budget and plows the savings into discounts for customers. Everyone can understand that concept and appreciate it, because everyone loves getting a discount more than seeing ads.

People are naturally curious about all three kinds of why—why this program, why them, why this special discount. If you can answer those, you'll be making great progress in your pitch. Next you'll be ready to move on to the *Pullback*.

42

Step 4: The Pullback

UP UNTIL NOW, your pitch has been drawing in the prospect, trying to get them more and more interested. But now we're taking a quick detour to what I call the *Pullback*. This tactic creates exclusivity, on the principle that you should aim to be the needed, not the needy (as we'll see in a few chapters).

During a Pullback you actually start to take away the wonderful program you just introduced, because it's not right for everyone, and not everyone qualifies. Heck, you might not let them buy it even if they want to.

This immediately drives two key mental shifts in your prospect. First, they will want to qualify, because everyone wants to feel special, to feel validated, to earn a gold star. Everyone is at least curious about benefits that aren't available to just anyone.

Second, and just as important, the Pullback reassures your prospect that you're not doing a hard sell, which further raises their trust level. You're clearly not willing to say or do anything to close them.

A good Pullback will briefly explain the rules of exclusivity for your program. "You will only qualify if you meet these four key requirements. . . ." Then add something like "If you qualify, that would be great, but if not, that's okay too. Maybe we can try again in the future. By then you'll see that a lot of your neighbors really like our program. Did I mention that Frank down the block qualified, and so did Mrs. Richards on Maple Street?" The unspoken subtext: *If you don't qualify, too, you're a loser!*

I once knocked on the door of a guy who was in a terrible mood. He kept saying, "I'm not interested," over and over—wouldn't even listen to my intro. So I immediately fast-forwarded to a Pullback: "That's okay, you probably wouldn't even qualify anyway." To be honest, I wasn't really hoping to close him, just messing with his ego as revenge for how stubborn he was being.

After I repeated a few times that he probably wouldn't qualify for our program, his angry face and tone shifted. "Wait a second. What do I need to do to qualify?" Boom!

I casually replied, "I have five qualifying questions that I have to ask every homeowner to see if they're a good fit for our program. Can I step in real quick and ask you those?"

His face and tone softened a little more. "How long will it take?"

"Just a few minutes. Want me to take my shoes off?"

"No you can keep 'em on."

Do you see how a Pullback can disarm a prospect who starts out in a defensive crouch? In this case, now that the cranky guy was finally listening, I was ultimately able to close him.

Some other quick lines that can be very effective during a Pullback:

"If it makes sense for you that's great, but if not it's no big deal to me."

"How about we just walk through the details real quick? If it's not for you, no worries, I'll get out of your hair."

"Only about one out of three people are a good fit for our program. So if you don't qualify, I hope you won't take it personally."

The Pullback can be really quick, but it's a powerful step that a lot of salespeople neglect to include. It will set you up well for your next step, a smooth transition beyond the pitching phase.

43

Step 5: The Transition

THE TRANSITION IS HOW you shift from your initial pitch into the next phase of your sale, whatever that requires. It might mean getting inside the prospect's home or office to present the details of your program. Or it might mean doing a demo of features and benefits. Or it might mean scheduling an appointment on the phone for an in-person presentation. Wherever needs to happen after that opening pitch will require a transition.

The challenge is that you don't want the prospect to feel like you just made a sharp left turn from the friendly chat you've been having so far. You want it to feel smooth and natural, not threatening or anxiety provoking.

The most common mistake at the transition is pausing at the worst possible moment. You might have done a great job with the pitch elements we've been talking about—the hook, the introduction, the why, the bandwagoning, and so on. You might have established rapport, trust, and curiosity. But if you pause at the transition, as if seeking permission to keep going, all that progress can go off the rails.

Salespeople pause because it's natural to feel a twinge of uncertainty or self-doubt at this point. They hear a voice in their heads: *Did my pitch work? Did I earn the right to keep going? Do I really have a shot at closing this person, or am I wasting my time?* We all crave validation to relieve that uncertainty. In a perfect world, the prospect would clap, nod vigorously, and say, "Great job, Sam! You aced the pitch! Now you get to level up and do your presentation!"

In the real world, however, your prospect has no interest in validating you—instead they're still evaluating you. So if you pause for their approval, you might as well be wearing a sign that reads I LACK SELF-CONFIDENCE. And then the prospect will subconsciously start to lose confidence in you. Your positive momentum can vanish in just a few seconds.

I call this moment between pitching and presenting *the gap*—and the key to "minding the gap" is *not pausing*. You have to think and act like *of course* your pitch was great, and *of course* the prospect is ready to move to the next phase. Assume validation rather than waiting for a signal to continue. If the prospect wants you to slow down or pause, the burden is on them to say that. So take a leap of faith and jump over the gap.

THERE ARE REALLY two thresholds you're crossing when you jump that gap: one is *information* and the other is your *physical presence*. Both can pose a psychological threat to the prospect.

Let's start with the information threshold. We're all taught to be careful with our personal information. No matter how well you've built rapport so far, you're still a stranger. The way to get around a reluctance to disclose information is to ramp up your requests gradually. Start with some questions that are so easy, they barely even feel like crossing a privacy barrier.

Suppose I'm pitching and I get to the pullback—"If this program works for you, great. If not, it's not a big deal." Then I continue immediately with my transition: "Let me jot down some basic info so I can figure out if you qualify." No pause to see if the prospect is nodding. I just assume that the pullback has made the prospect less defensive, because I'm clearly *not* doing a hard sell, not making any exaggerated promises. My words and body language are saying, *Dude, I don't really care if you buy from me or not. I'm just explaining an opportunity.*

Then I slide into asking for very basic, non-scary information. We're easing into a rhythm where each question leads naturally to the next. It's like a bag of potato chips; if you say yes to the first, it's really hard to say no to the second and third. Imagine what a prospect might be thinking during these questions:

"What's your address here?"

This guy can just look at my house number, so I might as well tell him.

"What's your last name?"

He already knows my first name and can google the rest from my address, so I might as well tell him.

"Phone number and email?"

I'm a little nervous that he might start spamming me, but my phone and email are already on the web, so I might as well tell him.

Before long you can ramp up to more sensitive questions: birthday, credit card, whatever you need.

NOW LET'S CONSIDER the physical threshold. Whether you're selling B2C or B2B, crossing the threshold of someone's home or office is a key step. Both are sacred—no one wants a threatening stranger in either their home or workplace.

So you might see the prospect standing at the doorway with very defensive body language, like they're literally protecting their personal space from an intruder. Pretty intimidating, right?

When I sense major resistance from someone's body language, I try to defuse it by getting on the same side instead of face-to-face. I'll take a step to be nearly side by side, point to something on my clipboard, and casually say, "Look at this, let me show you how it works."

Then it's natural to walk with them into their home or office as you keep talking.

If you feel nervous about walking in, remind yourself that you're doing them a favor by entering their personal space, to help them.

You can also project confidence by saying something that makes it sound completely natural to step inside. For instance: "Let me jot down some basic info to get you qualified and explain our program in more detail. Can I lean on this table, or should we move to the kitchen? This will only take five or ten minutes." Giving a homeowner a choice of living room or kitchen sounds like a respectful question— but of course either answer includes permission to be inside.

Another good question is "Do you want me to take my shoes off?" If you say that while wiping your feet on the doormat, you convey respect. It will be very hard for the prospect to be a jerk to you at this point, especially if you've been building early trust, rapport, and curiosity.

In some cases you can get inside by needing to look at something specific. When I was selling security systems and the prospect said they already had an alarm, I'd say, "What kind of panel do you guys have? Is it the one that's diamond shaped? Is it the TR or the SQ?" They usually had no idea but would offer to look. Then I'd say that it would be faster if I took a quick look myself. Suddenly I was inside the house, making a beeline for their security panel, and we've done the transition.

After you've crossed the threshold by using any of these tactics, you can return to chitchat to reinforce that you're friendly and trustworthy. Something like "What do you guys like to do for fun?"

IF YOU SELL on the phone rather than D2D, your transition might mean getting an appointment scheduled for an in-person meeting or demo. That's when you'll go from pitching to presenting.

As with a D2D transition, the key on the phone is to continue immediately from your pullback, without pausing to fall into the gap.

It's *not* "Would you like to schedule an appointment?" [pause]

It's "Let's get you scheduled for an appointment."

That subtle change from question to statement makes a huge difference.

After that statement, don't ask an open-ended timing question like "When's a good day for me to stop by?" Instead, narrow down the appointment with a series of simple questions with just two options each.

"I can be in your neighborhood Wednesday or Thursday, which one's better for you?" Let's suppose they reply, *Thursday*.

"Cool, do you prefer early in the day or late in the day?" *Later*.

"Great, I have open slots at four and six, which one should I block?" *Six*.

"Great, just give me your email and I'll send you a confirmation."

See that quick rhythm of Q and A? If you had started instead with an open-ended question ("When's good for you?"), it might take forever to nail down a date and time. The prospect might even lose interest and not schedule an appointment at all.

Don't be afraid to transition straight into the presentation, either, if that feels possible. Or to transfer your call to a closing specialist, if that's the way your company is organized. "Hold on real quick, let me grab one of my experts who can walk you through the details."

Regardless of what you're transitioning to, focus on making it smooth and seamless.

44

Blend Tenacity with Empathy

TENACITY IS IMPORTANT and powerful. But if you are *only* tenacious, you can come across as arrogant or desperate.

Empathy is important and powerful. But if you are *only* empathetic, you will get walked all over by your customers.

Lots of salespeople focus on developing one or the other, but they are *way* more powerful in combination. A true carnivore combines a relentless drive to close deals with genuine empathy and a desire to help their prospects. Those two goals are *not* opposites—they can reinforce each other! If you truly want to help people, you'll have a stronger motivation to keep going when it gets tough. And if you truly want to close as many sales as possible, you'll keep caring about people even when they annoy you, frustrate you, or even threaten you with bodily harm.

A great example of blending tenacity with empathy happened a few years ago, when I was selling solar. Fortunately, someone else from my company was shadowing me and caught it on video, or people might not have believed it really happened.

I knocked on a door, and a dude started aggressively yelling and cussing me out, including, "Get the f— off my property!" Then he literally slammed the door in my face, before I could even say more than a couple of words.

But instead of walking away, like most sane human beings, I re-knocked the same door. My thinking was, *Hell no, I'm not taking that from this dude.* I knew that he was livid enough to punch me in the face, but I didn't want to give him the satisfaction of scaring me off. I know there's a right time to take no for an answer and move on, but this didn't feel like that time. I wanted to win his permission to give him my pitch. If he listened to me and *then* said no, at that point I'd feel fine about moving on.

The guy looked shocked when he opened his door a second time and saw me still on his doorstep. "DID I NOT JUST TELL YOU TO GET OUT!! WHAT PART OF NOT INTERESTED DID YOU NOT UNDERSTAND?!"

But this time, while he was too stunned to slam the door again, I was able to get in more than a couple of words.

"Don't worry, we're not selling anything. Do you have a lot of people come by and try to sell you stuff? I know that's super annoying. We're just here running energy reports for your neighbors. We just did Susan a couple of houses down, and we don't want to leave you guys out. It's just a quick check of everybody's meter, but we wanted to let you know first. Then we can set up a time to drop off the report for you."

Now he was curious enough to ask what this was about. I explained that some homes in his area qualified for a low rate on our company's solar program, which could save them a ton of money, but other houses wouldn't be eligible because their electric consumption was too low.

By this point I could see that he wasn't merely curious but actually interested. So I kept talking. "Checking the meter and looking up the status is free, to see if your house qualifies. Takes about twenty minutes. We'll be back to drop off Susan's report around 6:00, so if you let us run your report, too, we can swing back and leave it for you. We just need some basic info to set it up. What's your name?"

And then we were off to the races. He let me take a picture of his last electric bill, to see how his energy usage would fit into our solar program. He agreed to see me again when I came back with the meter report so we could go over it line by line. By the end of my return visit, he had gone from nearly beating me up to signing up for our plan. He even offered me referrals to other people in town!

This deal only happened because of the combined power of tenacity and empathy. If I had given up after he originally cursed me out, obviously there'd be no sale. But if I had just re-knocked without showing empathy, that would have failed too. He needed to hear that I felt his frustration at having salespeople knocking. He was able to absorb my subtext:

> *I get that salespeople are annoying. Don't worry, I'm on your side. I'm not trying to bother you with some hard sell—I just want to let you know about an opportunity that might really help you. I care about you so much that I'm taking a chance that you might beat the crap out of me!*

Always remember both of these mantras:

> *I care enough about my prospects to make sure they have this valuable information.*

> *I care enough about myself to keep going rather than quitting too soon.*

45

Be the Needed
Not the Needy

THIS IS ANOTHER crucial principle of pitching: *Strive to be the needed, not the needy.* Neediness signals desperation, and everyone hates desperation. Think of any dating scenario, like a party or bar or matchmaking app. Even if you look attractive (or even smoking hot), potential dates will run the other way if your words and actions scream, "Pick me! Pick me!" People will wonder what's wrong with you that has made you so desperate.

If I knock on your door or cold-call you, of course you'll assume I'm needy. I need you to buy so I can make my commission and advance my career. So it's important not to start the conversation by *coming across* as needy. I don't want you to run away like a hot woman being hassled by an ugly dude at a party. That kind of behavior gives sales professionals in general a bad reputation.

My goal is to flip the script and break your expectations by sounding like you need me more than I need you. I'll try to sound casual and almost disinterested, like it doesn't really matter to me if you buy or not. Something like this:

> *Hi, I've been setting up a ton of people in this neighborhood with X. Demand is very high, but not everyone is a good fit for it. So I just wanted to find out if X might also be appropriate for you. If it is, that would be awesome, but we might discover that you're*

not a good candidate. I just need a few minutes to show you what we're doing and why so many people are loving it.

I'm not lying; there truly is no need for me to be desperate. This street or neighborhood is full of opportunities. If you don't want to buy from me, that really is just fine. I have an abundance mindset, and I know I can simply go sell your next door neighbor, or the woman across the street. I have total confidence in (1) my ability and (2) my product. I have so much conviction that no single rejection can dent my belief in what I'm doing. So if this isn't right for you, I'll say good-bye with a smile and move on.

But if you *do* find what I'm saying valuable, I know that's a win for you every bit as much as for me. You'll thank me for it, and I'll say, "You're welcome," because I just did something generous *for you*.

I'm definitely *not* going to say something desperate, such as "Thank you so much for buying! I really need this sale, it means so much to me!" That would send all the wrong signals. I'm not the needy, I'm the needed!

This is another mindset adjustment that might seem minor but can have a huge impact on your energy and success rate.

46

Selective Amnesia

SELECTIVE AMNESIA IS another mindset hack that's extremely helpful when you're pitching. It sucks to get shot down by any prospect, and a few strikeouts in a row can really shake your confidence. Especially if some of those rejections are personal—some version of "Leave me alone, you loser!"

So I got an idea from the classic movie *Men in Black*. I started to imagine that whenever I blew a pitch, Will Smith would pop out of the bushes in his black suit, holding his little silver memory zapper. Boom! Now my memory of those strikeouts was erased, and I could make my next pitch with high confidence and energy.

A roofing company in Texas once hired me to coach their sales team, so I took the entire team out to watch me sell D2D. I spent five hours in a row getting my face kicked in, just one rejection after another. By 7:30 p.m. I had zero closes. I'm sure some of those reps wondered why their boss was paying this clown to teach them how to fail at pitching.

But I used selective amnesia to reset my energy. I kept thinking, *I know I'm good at this. Forget the last rejection!* Then, finally, I got my first deal. Then a second. Then a third. Three closes in one shift was a great shift! When we knocked off for the night at 9:15, those reps could see the value not only of the skills I was teaching them, but also the power of persistence—and selective amnesia.

So let's say you're cold-calling a list of three hundred prospects and the first three hang up on you. You will be very tempted to think, *This list sucks! I'm going to strike out three hundred times!* Instead, take a deep breath and think for a second. You just talked to three people out of three hundred, which is literally just 1 percent of the list. Do you really think there won't be a single buyer among the next two hundred ninety-seven?

Instead, think of it like rolling dice. If you roll a three, what are the odds that you'll roll another three next time? Still only one out of six, even if you just hit ten of them in a row. So don't get hung up on hot streaks or cold streaks. Each pitch is a fresh new opportunity.

Lenny Gray, author of the Door-to-Door Millionaire books, says that if you contact one hundred prospects a day, you have the opportunity to make one hundred new first impressions every day. If you practice selective amnesia, the impression you make at door ninety-nine or cold call ninety-nine will be just as energetic and optimistic as the first one. And you'll have a huge advantage over reps who start each day with enthusiasm but then get beaten down by their strike-outs as the day continues.

Before I got the hang of this, I used to do really well at the start of each day, when my excitement naturally poured out and helped me close deals. But then the rejections would suck away my energy as the day went on, and by midafternoon I was mentally exhausted. My tone and body language basically signaled, *I know you're gonna be just like your neighbors and reject me, so I should save you the time and just leave now. Sorry to bother you.*

If you start feeling depressed and defeatist, that can easily become a self-fulfilling prophecy. So whenever you feel yourself heading down the wrong energy path, STOP. Take a five-minute break to reset. Jump up and down, listen to a song that pumps you up, or call a friend who always makes you laugh. Say a few affirmations. And imagine Will Smith showing up with his memory zapper.

Before long, your ninety-ninth pitch of the day will have the same energy as your first.

47

Pretend You Get Paid for Each No

WE JUST SAW HOW selective amnesia can help you shake off rejections. Another mindset hack that's just as powerful is imagining that you get paid for every no.

To simplify the math, suppose you're selling D2D and earn a $1,000 commission on every sale. Let's also suppose your closing rate is 5 percent—you close one sale for every twenty people you pitch. Five percent of $1,000 is $50. So you can think of every no as being worth $50, because it got you that much closer to hitting your twenty prospects.

This means you have no reason to feel great when you close but lousy when you strike out. Every new pitch equals $50 in your pocket, so that's a huge incentive to do another, and another, and another.

This is much more motivating than thinking your next $1,000 is trapped in a safe somewhere, and you need to close a sale to unlock the safe. If you visualize your money as waiting to be unlocked, you'll get more and more discouraged if you build up sixteen, seventeen, eighteen fails in a row. Instead, you can start to feel okay about each no as a step toward your goal.

You can also imagine yourself as a sculptor with a block of marble that you want to turn into a bust. It might take one hundred hammer hits to chip away at the marble. Does that mean success is credited only to the last hit? No, it's all of them together, even though no one will want the bust until you finish it. The tenth and fiftieth hits are just as important as the last.

A good physical reminder of this mindset is to fill one of your pockets with dimes when you start pitching. Every time you hear a no, move one dime to a different pocket. As that pocket starts to fill up, you'll feel more and more excited rather than discouraged.

Of course, you can also make up your own counting mechanism if you prefer. Whatever it takes to remind yourself that every no is not a failure, but a valuable step on the road to success.

48

Ingenuity

AS IMPORTANT AS PREPARATION IS, sometimes you have to go with seat-of-the-pants ingenuity and instinct. Some situations in your sales career will be too crazy to anticipate. You'll have to hone and trust your gut.

One of my most memorable closes ever came when I was first selling alarm systems in Dallas, when I was just eighteen. I walked up to a house where an older man was watering his front lawn. I started to introduce myself from maybe ten feet away, and he immediately replied, "Go away!" But I pretended I couldn't hear him and kept talking while I approached. "Excuse me, sir, sorry to bug you, but I wanted to let you know that—"

In midsentence he turned his hose on me, full blast. I was suddenly soaked and stunned. My training didn't say what to do if a prospect sprays you with a hose. My first instinct was to get away from this crazy guy as fast as possible.

But my second instinct, a second later, said, *He wants me to feel intimidated and run away. But I'm not going to give him that satisfaction.* So I ignored the soaking and kept talking, like it didn't even happen. I started telling him about our alarm system, and now he was the one looking stunned. "Hey! Did you not hear me tell you to go away? Are you that stupid?!" Then he sprayed me a second time.

This time I smiled and said, "Excuse me, sir, it's a hundred and ten degrees out. Would it be too much to ask to get one more spraying? Those are really helping me cool off."

I could see him get even angrier, because I wasn't letting him intimidate me. He soaked me one more time, then turned to go inside, saying, "That's it, I'm calling the cops!" He slammed the door behind him.

By this point I was wet as a dog from head to toe and wondering if he was serious about trying to get me arrested for trespassing. I considered fleeing again. But now my instinct told me to knock on the house next door. When that homeowner answered, I said, "Sorry I'm wet. Your neighbor just sprayed me with his hose. Do you like that guy? He seems like an interesting cat."

The neighbor replied, "He's a grumpy old man. He hates everyone." So now we were building instant rapport, sharing a laugh about Angry Hose Guy. Who knew that getting soaked could work as an icebreaker? Soon I was inside his house, explaining how our program worked. We got close to closing a deal. But then he had to answer another knock at his door, from a cop who said, "Excuse me, is there an alarm sales guy in your house?"

My prospect and his wife looked very worried. *Who is this sketchy kid we allowed into our home?* The cop pulled me outside and checked my permit, which was completely in order. He asked if I had been harassing the guy next door. I told him the full story, and that I hadn't done or said anything improper to Angry Hose Guy. Fortunately, he believed me. "Okay, you seem legit. You're free to go."

Again, my instinct kicked in. "Thanks, Officer, but I'm in a jam now and I could use your help. My customers just saw you pull me out of their house, so they think I'm a bad guy. Could you please go back with me and tell them I'm not a criminal?"

And he did! After the cop reassured the couple, I finished closing the sale. On my way out after they signed the contract, I put three extra signs for our company in front of my new customer's house, facing Angry Hose Guy's house. I left with a huge smile.

In a moment of angry rejection, the average salesperson will think, *Oh well, I lost.* But a carnivore will think, *How can I turn this situation around? If there's a wall in front of me, how can I go around it, or over it, or through it, or knock it down? There's gotta be a way past that damn wall, even if my script doesn't explain it.*

This story also shows the importance of micro-wins—little bits of good news you can focus on, even when there's no sale. Clearly, there was no way Angry Hose Guy would ever buy from me, but that didn't make our interaction a total loss. First, I could feel proud that I didn't let him humiliate me. I didn't run away crying. I didn't lose my temper and punch him in the face—which would have made my encounter with the cop *very* different. Then I used the soaking to establish rapport with his neighbor. Those were all micro-wins, and they would have felt good even if I hadn't closed the neighbor.

So try to practice thinking, *How do I turn this bad situation into at least a micro-win? How do I flip a negative into some kind of positive?* If you can do that, you can trust your gut even in a totally bonkers moment.

PART
SIX

Presenting

49

Introduction to Presenting

THIS SECTION OF THE BOOK is about the elements of a killer presentation. Of course the details will vary depending on what you're selling. Some industries require a really quick presentation, just five or ten minutes, while others require a much longer or multi-touch presentation.

Nevertheless, there's a powerful framework that can be adapted to just about any kind of presentation, whether you've got five minutes or three hours. It will help you focus on the prospect's needs and wants, so you can hold their interest rather than boring them with too many details. The key elements are:

- *The introduction*: Set proper expectations and build trust to ensure that the rest of the presentation will go smoothly. If you nail this intro, your odds of closing will go up dramatically.

- *The demo*: Going over features and benefits, focusing on those that really matter to *this particular prospect*. Your demo should be built around *problem-solution transitions*: uncovering a problem tied to each set of features so you can show how your offering solves that problem. You demo a feature, explain the problem, show how the feature solves it, then transition to the next one. For instance, in selling a car, don't just mention the engine's horsepower—talk about how valuable its quick acceleration can be in tricky driving situations.

- *The micro-closes*: We'll dig into closing later in the book, but your whole presentation should lay the groundwork by generating "micro-closes"—a series of small *yes* answers that eventually lead to a final big *yes*. I call this a *Yes Train* because your micro-closes can feel like a train gaining speed, until its momentum is nearly unstoppable. Start laying that train track as early as possible.

- *The wrap-up*: Show the customer what happens next—product delivery, installation, future communications, or whatever's required for next steps. This is vital, because if you leave them in the dark about all that stuff, they'll be more likely to have second thoughts and cancel, or maybe they'll give you a bad review and refuse to make any referrals.

My most important principle of presenting is that you have to have your key points *scripted* out, yet at the same time you have to be *adaptable*. You have to expect the unexpected and be ready to roll with it if you get an off-the-wall question or objection. If you can't learn how to improvise, even perfect memorization won't save you.

Now let's dive into the details of what makes an awesome presentation.

50

Presentation Essentials

LET'S TALK ABOUT what you need to bring to any kind of presentation, whether at a homeowner's kitchen table or the boardroom of a CEO. A lot of salespeople get cocky about how much information they have in their heads but then get tripped up because they didn't bring effective materials.

For starters, keep in mind that everyone has one of four main learning styles: visual, auditory, reading, and kinesthetic. (This is called the VARK theory, if you want to google it for details.) "Learning style" simply means someone's favorite way to absorb, process, and remember information. You need to be prepared to connect with all four groups:

- A visual learner, like me, loves graphics. I doodle to help me grasp concepts.
- An auditory learner does best when hearing new material.
- A reader obviously prefers reading.
- A kinesthetic learner prefers touching things, getting hands-on experience with physical objects.

You can engage visual learners by including illustrations on handouts or PowerPoint slides. This works whether you're in person or sharing a screen on Zoom. You don't have to be a great designer to make simple stick figures, Venn diagrams, or other graphics. You can even write them in real time on a portable whiteboard.

I like to laminate my illustrations into what we call a slick, which you can show to lots of people without having it fall apart from too much handling. An effective slick sums up some key facts in short bullets, along with a simple sketch. If your slick is blank on the reverse, you can flip it over and make notes on the back, for more reinforcement of key points.

One of your slicks or slides should focus on the cost of doing nothing. If the prospect doesn't buy, they will be forfeiting X—more revenue, time savings, an improved quality of life, or some combination. Whatever it is, spell it out with short bullet points and simple graphics.

You may need to create different types of visuals for different types of customers. For instance, suppose you're selling dietary supplements. Your presentation to an overweight, inactive customer will be very different from your presentation to a guy who's already shredded but still looking for an edge. So you should prepare very different slicks or slides for both groups.

Once you have all these materials prepped, keep in mind that an auditory learner will likely ignore your visuals and hang on your words instead. Don't take that personally—just be prepared to make your case without relying on the graphics.

A reader may simply ask to read your fact sheets. Again, don't take it personally. Just come prepared with simple, clear fact sheets.

A kinesthetic learner craves something to hold. If you're selling something physical like windowpanes, siding shingles, or solar panels, bring a sample to pass around. If you're selling something abstract, like B2B software, you'll need to be more creative with your materials. For instance, you might bring an old-fashioned Rolodex as a prop to stress how advanced your CRM software is.

For all four types, bring a pad and pen to take notes while you ask discovery questions. This signals that you're paying attention and respect your prospects enough to capture their answers.

Next, be prepared with appropriate referrals to impress your prospects. As we've discussed, people like to see themselves in others who already love what you're selling. So if you're pitching a small business with $1 million in revenue, show them five happy customers who used your software to grow from $1 million to $10 million. We call that building a bridge for the prospect. You want them to easily see themselves in referrals that build up your credibility and trustworthiness.

I like to create a binder filled with brief, signed testimonials from a lot of different customers. Then I can flip through the binder and just show off the ones that best match the profile of whomever I'm presenting to.

Another option is to create a video library of testimonials on your phone or iPad, instead of a binder. How impressive would it be for a visual or auditory learner if you say, "Let me show you three short videos I made with customers who are a lot like you."

Finally, your presentation arsenal needs to include a competitive analysis. Many customers would tell me they wanted to shop around and see what other companies were offering and at what costs. My best response was to pull out marketing materials from those competitors and do a comparison right on the spot. If they already had all the competitive details they needed, why wait? Let's do this deal now!

Compare that with a rep who acts like a deer in the headlights when asked about their competition. If you're selling Vivint alarms but can't explain what ADT is offering and how much they charge, you probably aren't closing this prospect.

The more time you invest up front in preparing all these materials, the higher your closing rate will be. Count on it.

51

Memorize or Improvise? Both!

IN MY SENIOR YEAR of high school, I applied for a job selling a food processor called the Quick Chopper 2000, by doing demonstrations in local stores. It sounded like fun and it would add to my income from painting street addresses on curbs.

The manager found out during my interview that I was a Mormon, and he hired me because his boss told him Mormons make good salespeople. He didn't realize that this reputation for sales skills is because many Mormons go on missionary trips to foreign countries, where they practice knocking on doors to spread their message. But I was only seventeen and hadn't done a missionary trip yet, so I didn't have that experience.

The Quick Chopper folks arranged for stores like Kmart to set up a booth and announce that there was going to be a demonstration of a great new food processor. The PA announcement and flashing lights would draw a crowd to my table, and then it was my job to show how it worked and make it look irresistible.

They gave me a four-page script to memorize that included every possible detail about the Quick Chopper. But at that point I had no experience memorizing someone else's script. When I knocked on doors and offered to paint an address on a curb, I was mostly relying on friendly chitchat, which came naturally. And my pitch was so basic that anyone could understand it. A lot of people said yes because I was a nice young man, and fixing the visibility of their address seemed like a good deal for a small cost.

In my youthful ignorance, I assumed that selling Quick Choppers could work the same way. I skimmed through the script but didn't come close to memorizing it. I figured I could wing it with my usual chitchat.

On my first day at that Kmart table, a bunch of shoppers came over to watch me make homemade salsa using the Quick Chopper. I was joking around, asking questions to get to know the customers, who were mostly moms. They laughed at my jokes and seemed impressed while I made the salsa. I thought, *This is great, they love me, I'm killing it. My commissions are gonna be huge.*

But then nobody bought a Quick Chopper. I got a few high fives but not a single sale. I shrugged it off. Day one is always the hardest, right?

The next day I came back and repeated the demo. Same laughs and high fives, but still no sales. Same thing on day three. By then I was really confused and worried. I'd been acting just like I did when selling all those curb addresses, but totally striking out. I had to tell my manager that I hadn't sold a single Quick Chopper in three days. He agreed to come watch me the next day to see if he could diagnose my problem.

After seeing me get the same crappy results, my manager pulled me aside. "Dude, you're charming and people like you, but you're not even close to following the script. Did you even try to memorize it?"

"Um . . . no."

"Go home and memorize the effing script! *You are not the star of this show!* The Quick Chopper is the star, and it's your job to make the star look good! Don't come back unless you've memorized it!"

That moment forever changed my approach to sales. I finally put the effort into memorizing the presentation details, and the next day my results finally turned around.

Yes, connecting with the customer on a human level is important. Yes, getting them to like you is important. But it's just as important to make them like the product, whether it's a $79 Quick Chopper or a $79,000 car. This requires memorizing all the details of features and benefits so you can sound authoritative when talking about them. You need the details to paint a vivid picture of the problem and then the solution to that problem. There's no substitute for that memorization.

A script is ultimately just another tool in your toolbox. It's not a magic solution—it only works if you use it properly to make the product sound amazing. The challenge is that it can also be bad if you lean on it too heavily and end up sounding like a robot. Customers *hate* talking to robots.

So you need to get good at *both* memorizing product details *and* learning when to trust your gut to go off script. As we've seen, sometimes you need to ditch the script to make a deeper connection with the customer and show true empathy for their needs.

Just remember that before you can decide to go off script, you

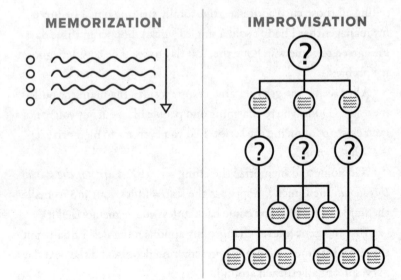

need to know the script. Memorize the key points, practice a natural way to say them, and then *hit those points every freaking time.* That rule has served me very well ever since my Quick Chopper days.

Years later, I got a valuable reminder from one of the best sales coaches ever, Myron Golden, who critiqued a pitch I was giving from the stage of a conference. He said, "Sam, your problem is that you're almost too good at improv. You're naturally witty and spontaneous, so you find it easy to go off on a tangent. Not everybody has that skill. But if you go too far off script, you can end up looping in circles and never get to the most important points you need to make. Your ability to riff becomes too much of a good thing. So write down your key points and memorize them word for word. Internalize them. Then watch what happens."

The next time I was pitching my company's training services from a keynote stage, I took Myron's advice. I memorized my key points but made them sound fluid and natural, not robotic. The best of both worlds. As a result of those relatively small changes, our training program's revenue boomed from about $150,000 to over $1 million.

The bottom line: Don't ever think you're too good to memorize a script. Memorize it, internalize it, and *then* be prepared to personalize it, when the moment calls for improv.

52

Don't Prejudge

I VIVIDLY REMEMBER one couple in Texas whose house stuck out from the rest of the neighborhood like a proverbial sore thumb. They had literal trash strewn on the front lawn. One of the front shutters was broken and dangling on its hinges. When I walked inside, the living room was cluttered with junk and smelled like cat urine. I concluded that they must have fallen on hard times, so I kept trying to head off price objections before they could raise them. When I got to the close, I explained how they could finance their $5,500 contract with small monthly payments over five years.

The husband then said, "How about if we just pay for the whole thing up front?" I was almost too shocked to reply while he casually wrote a check for the full amount. I later found out that they owned something like one hundred oil wells. I still don't know why they let their house get so run-down, but the problem must have been psychological, not financial.

As much as salespeople benefit by sizing up prospects quickly, it's dangerous to jump to conclusions. You can never be sure of someone's probability of buying from you, just because of factors like:

- Apparent income level
- Appearance

- Demographics (age, gender, ethnicity, etc.)
- Lack of early interest or engagement
- Lifestyle or type of home

I'm not saying you shouldn't notice such factors—those data points might help you. But you should disqualify anyone prematurely. Good prospects can look and sound like anyone.

You've heard on a million TV shows that the legal system presumes everyone is innocent until proven guilty. Likewise, you should presume that everyone is a good prospect until you have evidence that they aren't. Wait until they actually disqualify themselves, because they might not!

The antidote to prejudgment is asking questions. Start with a blank canvas and gradually fill in the blanks based on how they answer your questions.

For instance, suppose you start your presentation and the prospect says, "Well, you know, I'm not the type that usually buys on the same day." Don't jump to the conclusion that therefore you can't ask for his business today and it's pointless to continue. He did say *usually*, not *always*. This statement is useful information but not conclusive. After all, this person has never been sold by *you* before.

Or maybe you're well into your presentation and the prospect hasn't asked a single question or made a single comment. Yes, it's possible that they're simply not interested. But it's also possible that they're just intensely listening and thinking about everything you're saying. Maybe they just don't have any questions. You won't know until you know.

Or let's take a B2B example, where you're trying to pitch a small company with only six employees. You might prejudge that they're too small for the expensive software solution you're selling. But little do you know, they've just gotten venture capital funding of $100 million, and they're in the market for tools that can help them scale.

The takeaway from all these situations is that it's easy to shoot yourself in the foot by prejudging. Instead, psych yourself up and assume the best. Assume you can close *anyone* until you find out otherwise. Then let your presentation flow and see what happens. Otherwise you might be the one putting a kibosh on your own deals.

53

The Needs Audit

THE NEEDS AUDIT is a tactic that extends what we just learned about prejudging prospects too quickly. If you neglect to do a needs audit early in a presentation, you'll be shooting in the dark, trying to guess what the other person needs, wants, and cares about. But after a needs audit, you'll know *exactly* what targets you need to hit and where they are.

Remember my story about that terrible Ford salesman who failed to sell me a red F-150, even though I was dying to buy one? That's what can happen if you skip directly to assuming what a prospect is looking for. Instead of respecting my need to do a quick test-drive and then buy the exact truck I wanted, he jerked me around and dragged out the process. A total lose-lose outcome.

Never project your own preferences and values onto the other person. You might assume that if the roles were reversed, you'd focus on A, B, and C. But it's quite possible that your prospect has totally different priorities and expectations. If you don't find out ASAP, you can sabotage your shot at a deal. So within the first few minutes of your presentation, start asking questions that will reveal the following:

- How much they already know about your offering
- Why they decided to meet with you

- What questions they hope you will address
- What other options they might be considering
- What they would consider a deal-breaker, such as a certain price level or absence of certain features

Here are some examples of how a needs-audit conversation can go.

Me: "Hey, I appreciate you for taking the time to sit down with me. What was the main reason you decided to meet with me?"

Them: "I don't know."

This tells me the prospect is starting from scratch, so that's where I need to start my presentation. They haven't put much or any research into this subject, so I can't assume a baseline of understanding.

On the other hand, that same question might be answered with: "Well, we've been looking into buying X for the last six months, and we've already researched three other options and got price quotes. You're the last option we're considering before we decide."

That's a very different scenario! This prospect already knows the basics and a lot more. They will have detailed questions about features and pricing. So I'm not going to bore them with the basics. I'm going to focus on why we're different and what makes us better than our competitors.

Another good question you can ask at the top: "Hey, before I get started, I'm sure you already have thoughts on this. So what questions do you hope I'll cover? I want to make sure I hit every issue that's important to you."

Them: "We just want to know how much it is." Okay, so my presentation needs to be all about price versus value. Got it.

Or, conversely: "Our friend bought from your company, and told us he had concerns about X and Y. So we really need to be comfortable about those issues before we can commit." They just did you a big favor by flagging those potential problems. Now you can adjust your presentation to deal with them.

There's a saying that I love that applies here: "Spend 90 percent of your time sharpening the ax and 10 percent chopping the tree." Your needs audit is a great way to sharpen your ax. Take as much time as necessary with it, because it will pay off in a big way. The last thing you want to do is try to impress customers with things that aren't important to them.

54

Value = Emotion + Logic

YOU'VE PROBABLY HEARD the old saying "People buy emotionally but justify logically." If you fail to bring in the emotional aspect, you will find it difficult to build urgency. But if you fail to bring logic in, you may find yourself facing endless objections and price battles.

So your goal is to get both emotions and logic working together to point your prospect toward buying. Emotion plus logic creates more value than either one separately.

Let's say you're in the mood for a hamburger and I'm selling burgers for twenty-five dollars each. You might respond by saying my burgers are way overpriced, because you can get a McDonald's burger across the street for just two dollars.

But what if we change the scenario? Suppose you haven't eaten anything in two days, and the nearest McDonald's isn't across the street, it's fifty miles away. Suddenly twenty-five dollars for my burger sounds like a great deal! In fact, you'd probably pay fifty dollars, because you're starving! The logic of needing food combines with your emotional desperation to scramble your normal calculation of value. Maybe the next day you'll kick yourself for spending twenty-five dollars, but right now my burger is irresistible. It depends on your personal definition of value at that moment.

As a salesperson, you need to be prepared to make both logical and emotional arguments, depending on what you learn about the prospect. In this example, if they let slip that they're starving, I can use that information. I might say, "Hey, I respect that you think my burger is overpriced. This time of day you can drive to McDonald's in about two hours. And they might already be closed if you hit traffic."

For other customers, you might have to get into the details about the quality of your beef compared with McDonald's beef. What's the fat content? The USDA rating? Your average ratings on Google and Yelp?

For a third group of customers, what really matters is how much the cows who provide the hamburger meat had to suffer. These folks have strong emotions about the ethical treatment of animals. So you might stress that McDonald's is known to abuse its cows, while yours are free range and are treated humanely throughout their lives.

As you craft your presentation, think about what heartstrings you can pull on emotionally and what brain strings you can pull on logically. Then adjust your approach based on what you learn from asking questions.

If you can get a combination of both emotions and logic on your side, even a twenty-five-dollar burger will look like the best deal in town.

55

The Pre-frame

SETTING EXPECTATIONS should be a key part of the intro to your presentation. This starts with the basics, like telling the prospect how long it will take and inviting them to interrupt at any point with questions. This is also a good time to mention your company's story—here's what we do and what we stand for. That can reassure them that you're legit and your goal is happy customers.

After those preliminaries, slide into what is called a pre-frame. This is a blunt warning that the purpose of this presentation is to reach a clear decision. At the end you're expecting them to commit to a yes or a no, but not a maybe. Your pre-frame touchpoints in delivering this message may include:

- I'm going to go over our **program/product**.
- I'm going to explain our **pricing**.
- I'm going to walk you through our **process**.
- I'm going to answer all your **questions**.
- I'm going to ask you to reach a yes-or-no decision today.

Example: "So, Mr. Customer, I'm about to go over how this all works, our pricing, our process, and answer all of your questions. Then you should have all the info you'll need to come to an educated decision today. Whether you decide that this makes sense for you or not, I'll respect your decision. Sound fair?"

If you fail to pre-frame, the prospect may assume you're just giving them an education and answering questions, with no obligation in return. Then there's a good chance that you'll finish your presentation and hear something like "Thanks, that was really informative. Can I have your card? I need to think about it and get back to you."

So you have to set your intention at the top, before you get into the nitty-gritty. This isn't a hard sell; you can be clear that you'll respect a no answer, after they hear all your information and ask all of their questions. In return, all you're asking for is a clear decision one way or the other. If you do your job properly, they should have 100 percent of the info they need to decide.

At the end of the presentation, you can refer to the pre-frame if the customer tries to kick the can. Remind them that you had an agreement. You're willing to keep answering questions if they still have more questions. You're also willing to move on if this isn't right for them. But if they're still undecided, ask what they still need.

"Does the product make sense for your needs? Is the price fair? If those answers are yes, why can't we move forward? What else do you need to move forward? I want to be fair to you, but I also hope you'll be fair with me. So please help me understand what you're thinking at this point."

This gives you an advantage, because you're transferring the burden of proof to your prospect. You're taking away their option to procrastinate. If they're on the fence between yes and no, a good pre-frame can give you ammunition to tip them over to yes.

56

Building Rapport without Landing in the Friend Zone

RAPPORT IS SIMPLY a word for how well you're getting along with your prospect during your presentation. Everyone knows it's a good thing. But many don't realize that it's possible to develop *too much* rapport. My term for that is *getting stuck in the friend zone*—and it can be a killer.

I've mentioned repeatedly how important it is to build points of connection with a customer, by bonding over anything you have in common. That might include chatting about your kids, hometown, hobbies, or shared love for F-150 trucks. We've seen how personal bonding questions can defuse tension and help you overcome objections.

The key is to keep it light, fun, and *not too long*. Sales reps get into trouble when their insecurity or anxiety takes over, and they try too hard to be liked. If you go down conversational rabbit holes, prospects may start to feel like you're wasting their time. Their image of you will slide from a serious sales professional to just some person who's trying to be friends. Then their sense of urgency will probably evaporate.

I've fallen into this trap myself, too many times. As a consultant, I end up spending a lot of time with my clients. The more we hang out together, the harder it can be to maintain a professional tone. At some point it gets too awkward to ask for full price for my services or speak up assertively about an overdue payment. Whenever I accidentally cross into the friend zone, it's hard to reset our original boundaries.

For instance, I once had a client named Jefferson who signed a six-figure annual contract for sales consulting. I helped him grow his business from $1 million to $20 million in revenue, and I loved hanging out with him. I admired him as an entrepreneur, to the point that he almost felt like a big brother (he was ten years older). I started inviting him to my private parties and golf outings with nonwork buddies.

Sounds like a dream client, right? Well, when it was time for Jefferson to renew his contract after two years, he canceled it instead. Why should he pay all that money to get advice from a friend?

You have to assume that your prospects aren't dumb. They know you're trying to sell something. They know you're trying to forge a connection that will serve your needs, not because you literally want to be their friend. And they will usually go along with that kind of chitchat, but only up to a point. So try to toggle back and forth between building rapport and keeping your exchanges professional.

For instance, suppose you find out that a prospect recently took his family to Hawaii, your favorite place in the world. Of course you should pause to share your love for Hawaii. It's fine to ask where they went and what was the highlight of their vacation. Just don't go off on that tangent for more than a minute. Bring it back to your presentation about the value you're offering.

The same is true for telling your own story as a means of building rapport. It can help to *briefly* share why you're doing this kind of sales and how you got into it. These disclosures can build your credibility while inviting prospects to become part of your world. You'll seem more like a real person, not some anonymous sales robot.

For instance, you can say something like "I got into this business about six years ago—a long time, right? I'm passionate about helping our customers because I believe in our product so deeply. I'm also trying to get promoted to assistant sales manager. So I really appreciate that you're meeting with me. Every chance I get to help someone like you brings me closer to a promotion."

But be careful to share your personality and personal story only in small doses. That's how you'll stay on track toward a close instead of getting stuck in the friend zone.

57

The Problem-Solution Transition

DURING THE MAIN PART of your presentation, focus on what we call *the problem-solution transition*.

Start by painting a vivid picture of whatever problem the customer is facing. Use a blend of stories and facts that will have an emotional impact. Then immediately transition to the features of your product that will solve the problem. A great presentation might go back and forth three or four times: problem → solution, problem → solution, and so on. You might spend five to ten minutes on each, so this part of your presentation might take fifteen to forty minutes total.

Let's look at three examples in different fields.

When I sold alarms, I used to ask, "What concerns you more, a home invasion type one or a home invasion type two?" Most people don't know this police lingo, so they would ask what the difference was. I'd explain that type one is a break-in when the resident is home, maybe asleep or just chilling in the kitchen. Type two is when you come home to a break-in that's already in progress, and you catch the bad guys off guard.

Was explaining these awful scenarios an unfair scare tactic, because customers would always mentally fill in the blanks? I don't think so. I was just giving facts to paint a vivid picture of different potential problems. Then I'd show how our alarm system could protect them from both types of home invasions. **Problem → solution.**

Now picture a realtor showing a fixer-upper to an eager couple. "The problem with an old house like this is that you'll need to spend at least forty grand on upgrades before you move in, including the floors and the kitchen. It would be a big mess to wait to do those renovations later. But doing them now will be a huge hit to your savings, and it will take years before you recover it in equity. Instead, you could put that forty grand into a bigger deposit on a new house that doesn't need renovations. That would pay off in increased equity right away." (The unspoken additional point: a realtor gets no commission on renovations.) **Problem → solution.**

Or imagine a pet store owner with a family shopping for a new puppy. First, the problem: "Most people fall in love with a cute puppy but have no idea how long it will take to train them and how hard it's going to be. Six months later, they're still finding poop and pee and vomit on their floors and furniture. They still have to take the puppy out four times a day, and they become resentful. They feel dumb for getting into this situation in the first place."

Now, without pause, the solution: "We have an awesome service where we take the puppy back three weeks after you get him and start to bond with him. We do a professional two-week training that guarantees he will come back to you potty-trained and knowing a few basic voice commands. So your tough time will only last three weeks, not six to nine months. We know that a well-trained dog equals a great family pet experience, and the best time to train them is when they're this young. Can't teach an old dog new tricks, right? And of course we'll take care of all their necessary immunizations and give you the right nutrition plan."

This solution is so appealing that it's easy to do yet another transition, directly into a closing. "Nine out of ten of our customers sign up for this service because it solves all the headaches of a new puppy. So the next steps are really simple. I'll take down your information for our onboarding process and explain what you need to do during those first three weeks. And of course we want to make sure you fully understand everything, so we'll answer as many questions as you might have. Now let's start with your name, address, phone, and credit card information. . . ."

The key to this transition is not pausing, as we discussed earlier about "minding the gap" during an initial pitch. Pausing for the customer to agree or signal approval is a sign of insecurity. Don't wait, because *of course* they will want this awesome solution to the problem you've painted for them.

Problem → solution → closing.

58

The Pain Tunnel

THE BETTER YOU ARE at uncovering people's problems and making those problems feel intense, the more fluid your presentation will be, and the more likely that you will close. That's why the problem-solution transition works so well, as we just saw.

An especially strong version of this tactic is what I call *the pain tunnel*. Imagine dragging the prospect into a dark, scary, claustrophobic tunnel where their problems are right in their face. Ask more questions than you may think necessary to identify specific pain points and exactly what your prospect hates about them. Only after the tunnel has really gotten to them do you lead them out the other side, into a far better place with sunshine and rainbows.

It's one thing to talk about a problem in the abstract, but something else to really stew in the details and potential consequences of that problem. Imagine going to your doctor and he says, "Hey, you ought to quit smoking." You already know this intellectually, so you shrug it off. But now imagine that your doctor shows you graphic pictures of people dying from lung cancer and emphysema. That's the power of the pain tunnel.

Think about the worst-case scenario of how a problem might escalate if the customer turns down your solution. For instance, if you sell life insurance, you can describe a family left with no financial security after the father died in a tragic car accident. Walk through the

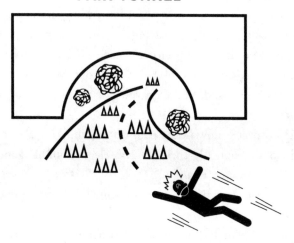

details of the emotional and financial stress of those devastated family members. Then and only then, pull your customer out of the tunnel and show how your solution can make everything better. In this case, you can describe another family where the same car accident didn't lead to financial ruin, because the father had bought enough insurance to protect his loved ones.

Here's another, less morbid example. When I used to do solar presentations, I'd try to make the pain of a prospect's electric bill feel real and immediate. Most people stop paying attention to the bills they pay month after month. They go on autopilot, and often on autopayment. Zero thought equals zero pain. So I'd use an analogy: "Imagine that instead of buying your house twenty-five years ago, you started renting it. Imagine that every month you paid your landlord, but with nothing to show for it in equity. Your landlord captured all the appreciation in the house's value, then sold it and kicked you out. How would you feel about that?"

Them: "Well, I'd feel really stupid for renting all those years instead of buying. I would never do that. That's why I own my house."

Me: "Exactly—you'd never waste all that money on rent. But guess what, that's exactly what you've been doing all these years with your electric bill. You've been paying the power company month after month, with nothing to show for it! Imagine if you could have set up a way to get free electricity instead. What could you have done with those tens of thousands of dollars you gave the power company over the years?"

The prospect is now in the pain tunnel, thinking about all that wasted money. Suddenly, their monthly electric bill has gone from a no-brainer to a source of anguish.

Before I let them out of the pain tunnel, I'll add another tactic called *imagine if*.

"Imagine if you don't do anything to change your electricity over the next five years. Two hundred dollars a month equals $2,400 a year equals $28,800 in five years! What could you do with an extra twenty-nine grand in five years?"

Imagine if is powerful because most people live from week to week, never stopping to consider what might happen in five years based on today's decisions. So if you paint a clear picture of future pain, you can turn it into a vivid and *immediate* problem. Then the prospect will be thinking, *Please get me out of this situation!*

That's when you pull them out of the tunnel and continue with the rest of your presentation. They will be a lot more receptive to your solution now that they've really *felt* how much money they've already wasted—and how much more they might potentially waste in the future.

59

The Inception Shovel

LOOK AT THIS PICTURE—two people but only one shovel. Would you rather be the guy who's digging the hole and sweating bullets, or the guy up on top, cheerleading?

INCEPTION SHOVEL

The same unbalanced division of labor happens in most presentations. The sales rep is digging nonstop, working super hard, stuck in the pit. They're giving all the answers with nonstop *talking, talking, talking.* Then the rep reaches the gold at the bottom and turns to the prospect for approval, but the person on top has already checked out mentally. They haven't invested any labor in reaching the gold, so they can take it or leave it. They often say they need to think it over before deciding.

To avoid this scenario, I came up with a presentation technique I call *the inception shovel.* It's named for the Leonardo DiCaprio movie where scenes are implanted inside people's dreams, and make the people believe things they wouldn't normally believe because of those dreams.

The key to this technique is a famous saying: "People love to buy, but they don't like to be sold." The best kind of selling is when you make the prospect connect the dots on their own so they feel like buying is their idea, not yours. In other words, give them the shovel and let them dig their own hole to reach the gold. Then they'll be excited instead of indifferent.

You can create an inception shovel by asking certain kinds of open-ended, conversational questions that steer the prospect toward the conclusion you want, without their realizing how much you're influencing that conclusion. This may require holding back your instinct to be super assertive and bombard your prospect with a ton of facts and figures. You can go back to the chapter on the four types of questions for a refresher on open-ended questions that lead people in a certain direction.

Consider two ways of presenting the same information about what makes my company legit and trustworthy.

First, here's me doing all the digging myself: "Our company has three hundred fifty reviews on Google, with a four point seven star rating. We've been rated A plus with the Better Business Bureau. We have a bunch of accolades on our website, just let me pull them up and show you. We have seven features that our customers really love, let me go through them now. . . ."

Can you visualize the other person's eyes glazing over?

Instead, here's a typical dialogue of what happens if I hand over the shovel:

ME: "I'm sure you'd be skeptical if I just told you how wonderful our company is. Of course I think so—I wouldn't work for them if I didn't. But let me ask you, what do you consider important when evaluating a company? What would make you feel good about us? Is it mainly online reviews, or endorsements from former customers, or . . . ?"

THEM: "Well, I like to see that a company has at least a four-star rating online. And some positive customer reviews."

ME: "Sure, that makes sense. Do you use Google to find reviews?"

THEM: "Yeah, I'd google it."

ME: "Great. So how many customer reviews would you consider reliable, if the average rating is over four stars? Do you think like thirty, fifty, one hundred, two hundred reviews, or what?"

THEM: "I'd say one hundred reviews is a good number, if the average is over four stars. Maybe 4.2 stars."

ME: "That's fair. Can you do me a favor and pull out your phone and google us?"

THEM, AFTER GOOGLING: "You guys have three hundred fifty reviews with a 4.7 average."

ME: "Yup! Isn't that cool? It's way better than you said you needed to think we're reputable. That's why I love my job so much—our customers love us. There's a lot of crappy companies out there, and I'm so glad to work for one of the best."

The key moment was when I planted the idea that a good company would have between thirty and two hundred customer reviews, and I asked the prospect to pick a standard to evaluate. I knew they'd probably say one hundred or two hundred, and I knew they'd be much more impressed by our three hundred fifty than if I had just revealed that number off the bat. The prospect had probably never considered how many reviews were a reliable standard, until I incepted that concept. Then it suddenly felt like *their own* personal standard.

That's the power of the inception shovel. You can do this with every element of presenting your problem and solution. Look for every opportunity to stop talking, ask open-ended questions, and guide the prospect to find the answers themselves. Then the *aha* conclusion—that they really want to buy—will feel like their idea, not yours.

PART SEVEN

Objections

60

Introduction to Objections

IF YOU CAN'T DEAL with objections, you can't sell, period. Some days you'll get a few. Some days you'll get a ton. But you'll *never* have a day without any objections.

I remember knocking doors once when it felt like someone must have called every single house in that neighborhood and bribed them to be jerks to me. I would barely get my first sentence out and the response would be "Not interested!" followed by a slammed door.

But here's a fact that kept me sane that day, and a lot of other days when I kept getting kicked in the face. If someone says, "Not interested!" before they even know what you're selling, that's not really an objection—it's a smoke screen. Knowing the difference between the two is absolutely essential. You're going to learn it in this section of the book, along with some powerful tactics to overcome *smoke screens*, *true objections*, and a third category I call *conditions*.

In retrospect, on that terrible day I was probably just projecting negative energy. I should have taken a break to reset. Instead, I kept going and did an experiment to try to break my cold streak. I took out a hundred-dollar bill and started holding it up while I used a new opening line: "Hi, I'm Sam, and I'm in your neighborhood today to give away one hundred dollars, if you'll just answer three simple questions."

Sadly, I couldn't even get the next five homeowners to listen to my questions to score some easy cash. If any of them had gone along with it, they would have heard me quote the bridge keeper scene from *Monty Python and the Holy Grail*: "What is your name? What is your favorite color? What is your quest?" Oh well, their loss!

These days I feel so confident in my ability to handle objections that I'm a little disappointed when I don't get any. I'll think, *Wait a minute, come on, hit me with something!*

Here's another reason why you should think of objections as valuable. Nine times out of ten, if a prospect doesn't raise a single objection, they aren't really listening. They've checked out, and when you get to the end, they'll say something like "Oh, that's great. Thank you. Can you leave me some information? I'll call you if I'm interested."

I love this quote by Bo Bennett: "An objection is not a rejection; it is simply a request for more information." If you can fill that request, you have no reason to fear objections!

So let's get into it. . . .

61

Deal-Breaker, Smoke Screen, or True Objection?

THE FIRST THING YOU NEED to do when hearing pushback is to figure out if the customer is giving you a deal-breaker condition, a smoke screen, or a true objection. If you misdiagnose the pushback, you'll end up responding with the wrong tactics, and they probably won't work. It's like trying to use a screwdriver on a flat-head nail.

A *deal-breaker condition* is a problem that truly can't be solved or overcome. For instance, suppose you're selling a service that can be purchased only by a homeowner. You start talking to a prospect, and within a minute you find out that they aren't the homeowner, they're just renting the house for a few months. That means they are literally disqualified from buying from you. The same is true for the following situations:

- The person has terrible credit and can't get approved for financing.
- They're in bankruptcy right now.
- They're planning to move soon.
- They're already in contract with one of your competitors.

There's nothing you can do about any of these, so just excuse yourself and move on. Don't waste your time, and don't get discouraged.

A *smoke screen* can be a little harder to confirm, but the usual tell is that the pushback comes within the first minute of starting your pitch. It's just an excuse to make you go away, because this person simply doesn't feel like listening to you right now. Their pushback has no connection to what they might think of your offering if they gave you a fair chance to sell it.

The most common smoke screens are:

- *I'm not interested.*
- *I need to talk to my spouse or partner first.*
- *I'm too busy to talk now.*
- *I can't afford it.*
- *I'm already happy with my current [whatever].*
- *I need to do my own research before talking to any reps.*

You can usually blow away all of these, like smoke, using some techniques we're going to cover.

However, if a prospect repeats a more substantial concern over and over, it might be a *true objection*. For instance, some people really do delegate all purchases to their spouse. In that case you might really need to reschedule for when the spouse is home.

Other true objections will come later in the conversation, after the prospect has given you enough time to explain what you're pitching. These need to be taken seriously and answered in depth. Maybe you can solve them if you and the prospect dig into the details together and treat it like a joint challenge.

For instance, if you're pitching a fitness coaching service and trying to get the prospect to see the value in personalized coaching sessions, they might reply, "I just follow an online workout plan and it works for me." That's a true objection, not a deal-breaker or a smoke screen. It's an invitation for you to make the case for your service: Why should this person spend extra money for personalized coaching? If you can make a good case that your service adds more value than whatever solution they're currently using, and is worth the extra cost, you have a real shot at winning their business.

A true objection is exactly the kind of pushback you *want* to hear. It's a fastball over the plate; you just need to learn how to hit it.

62

Selective Hearing

SELECTIVE HEARING SIMPLY MEANS choosing which objections or smoke screens you will pay attention to and how you will respond to them. These are actually two separate questions. You can decide to completely ignore pushback if you think it's a smoke screen, and just keep going with your pitch. Or else you can acknowledge the pushback but feed it into an imaginary translator machine to convert it into a solvable objection. In other words, the prospect says X but you hear it as Y, then respond to Y.

Let's see how this works with three common D2D examples.

Say I'm selling solar panels, and within the first thirty seconds, the prospect says, "Sorry, I'm broke, I can't afford this." This is almost certainly a smoke screen, because it's so early in the pitch. I haven't even gotten a chance to explain that it will cost zero out of pocket, saving the customer money from day one. So it makes no sense for them to say they can't afford it.

I therefore choose not to hear this objection at all. I think this person has been programmed to push away any kind of salesperson, but that brush-off won't work on me. Instead of arguing back about why they actually can afford it, I let the smoke screen go in one ear and out the other. Then I say, "That's okay. Anyway, so what we're doing is . . ." and I keep going.

This is called a *micro-validation*—a simple acknowledgment that takes no more than two seconds before you move on. It puts me back in the driver's seat and buys me more time.

Another option for addressing this smoke screen is to feed it into the translator. When I hear "I can't afford this," I instantly translate it to "Show me how I *can* afford this." So I respond with "That's exactly why I'm here, to show you why everyone is doing this." This doesn't merely defuse the objection—it flips it into a *reason* to keep listening.

Here's another common smoke screen: a stay-at-home mom says, "I need to talk to my husband first." I put that through my objection translator and it comes out as "Please show me how I can do this without my husband." Same idea, but now it's a solvable problem.

My reply: "Oh, I totally get it. We're going to make this super simple and totally affordable. Let me go through the details with you now. I bet when you tell him about it later, he's going to be thrilled."

One more classic smoke screen: "I'm too busy to talk now." Many salespeople hear that as a no—but the word no never came out of their mouth! My objection translator turns it into "Whatever I'm busy with at the moment—my job, my kids, the laundry—feels more important than whatever you're selling."

That's a solvable objection, and totally fine! I'll reply with something like "Totally, I'll make it super quick and be out of your hair before you know it." That gives her a micro-validation to show that I heard her.

Selective hearing not only gets around smoke screens; it also improves your mindset. If you take every kind of pushback at face value, you'll just hear *no, no, no*—and you'll feel like you're getting beat up the whole time. But unless they literally use the word *no*, just keep going. "I'm busy" isn't a no. "I need to talk to my spouse" isn't a no. The translator turns them into solvable objections. You won't overcome every one of those objections, but at least you'll have a fighting chance.

Think of it like being a quarterback under pressure. Don't assume you're going to be sacked until you're actually on the ground. Maybe you can still get the pass off. Maybe you can scramble and pick up a first down. If you stay cool, there are ways to get around the defense!

In the next few chapters you'll find several more techniques that defuse real objections, not just smoke screens.

63

The 8-Mile Technique

THIS IS MY FAVORITE WAY to deal with objections. I got the idea years ago from the classic Eminem movie *8 Mile*. (If you've never seen it, see it! It's an epic sales movie as much as a hip-hop movie.) The 8-Mile technique has worked for everyone I've ever taught it to.

The climax of the movie is the final rap battle. Papa Doc wins the coin toss and elects to let Rabbit (Eminem) go first. Aware that his opponent has a lot of ways to mock and attack him, Rabbit unloads a bunch of negative information about himself, to steal the other guy's thunder in front of the crowd. For instance, he raps:

> *This guy ain't no m——g MC,*
> *I know everything he's got to say against me!*
> *I am white, I am a f——g bum,*
> *I do live in a trailer with my mom . . .*
> *I did get jumped by all six of you chumps!*
> *And Wink did f— my girl!*

This goes on for a while, and then Rabbit ends with:

> *Here, tell these people something they don't know about me!*

What can Papa Doc (real name: Clarence!) possibly come back with to dis Rabbit? He has to concede defeat.

You can do the same during your pitch or presentation, addressing the objections you expect to hear before the prospect has a chance to get them out. You might leave your listener just as speechless as Papa Doc. Start by preparing for the common smoke screens we covered earlier:

- *I know I'm not interested.*
- *I know I can't afford it.*
- *I've already talked to people like you before.*
- *I don't need help with this problem.*
- *I'm too busy to talk.*

Then keep going, listing the most serious objections you've ever heard about your product.

Let's say I'm selling a pest control service. I'll start to 8-Mile early on, especially If I've been hearing the same few objections lately from other homeowners, and especially if this prospect's body language is signaling resistance. For instance:

> *"Hey, I bet you've probably already talked to five or six guys trying to pitch you on pest control, right? Those bug guys are annoying, aren't they? Nobody likes door-to-door salespeople! Plus, I bet you've been trying to save money these days, with inflation so bad, am I right? Yeah, me too. I hate wasting money on anything I don't need. That's why I'm so glad my company is doing something totally different. I'll be super quick because I can tell that you're busy, right? That's good because I need to leave soon anyway, because I have an appointment with Susan down the block. But before I run, let me show you this cool program we're running. . . ."*

Boom, boom, boom—I just covered all the major potential smoke screens in about ten seconds.

"I'm busy." *That's great, I'm busy, too, and I need to run soon anyway.*

"I already talked to five other bug guys." *Aren't those guys annoying, always pushing the extended warranties? I hate that. That's why we're nothing like those jerks.*

The key to a great 8-Mile is preparation. Take notes on every smoke screen or serious objection you hear, or those you gather from more experienced reps at your company. Then practice bringing those objections up before the prospect even has time to say them. By paying attention to the other person's body language, you can often guess what objection is on the tip of their tongue, such as "I'm too busy." Practice weaving your response lines into the conversation naturally so it sounds like you just came up with them off the top of your head.

This may take a while to get the hang of, but it's totally worth the effort. When you get good at using 8-Mile, an observer shadowing you might say something like "Wow, you're getting all the nicer customers today." Actually, my customers aren't any nicer or meaner than anyone else's. I'm just disarming them with the 8-Mile technique. I'm taking their objections out of their hands and giving myself a lot more time and breathing room to finish my pitch.

And as a bonus, I wind up getting beaten up by prospects a lot less often.

64

Objection Fence Staking

OBJECTION FENCE STAKING is similar to 8-Mile, but this technique is built right into your presentation to neutralize potential concerns and problems. The metaphor is to put an imaginary fence around each objection you anticipate so it can't break loose and start causing havoc.

First you need to get inside the minds of your customers and predict which objections they are most likely to bring up. Then think

OBJECTION FENCE STAKING

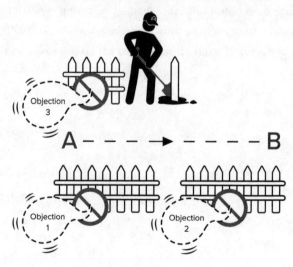

about what answers are mostly likely to satisfy them. Then script those talking points *early in your presentation*, ideally before most prospects would even raise those objections. Then practice your scripted lines until they sound smooth and natural. If you stutter and stumble because you feel defensive about an objection, you'll lose credibility.

The power of this technique is that you're not waiting around for the customer to raise the objection. You're taking the initiative and showing them how well prepared you are.

For instance, imagine a homeowner who says they need to compare multiple bids before choosing a vendor for a home upgrade. Because you've done your homework, you have the facts in front of you about competitive pricing. You can stake the fence by saying something like "That's a smart idea. Most people in your shoes want to see a competitive analysis. I've brought a few similar recent bids from other customers in this area so you can see what our competitors are charging. Would it be helpful for you to review those? Or do you just trust me on this?"

Whatever you're selling, people are likely to have objections about money, about feeling pressured into a decision, and about disliking change. So I built my presentations around those three common concerns, and turned each into a reason to move forward.

As an example, here's how I use fence staking these days when I sell high-ticket B2B sales coaching services.

Objection: "I can't afford this."

- How can you expect your own customers to buy big-ticket items from you, if you're afraid to buy something similar yourself?
- Our coaching is an investment, not an expense. Our clients consistently reach new levels of revenue, so our coaching usually pays for itself.

- One of the biggest dangers for any entrepreneur is a scarcity mindset. If you expect money to be so tight that you can't invest in yourself, that will be a self-fulfilling prophecy. You need an abundance mindset instead. You can definitely earn enough to afford our coaching!

Objection: "I hate making decisions."

- We know that decisive people sell more. You can train yourself to be more decisive. It will make your whole life easier and your company more successful.
- You're not alone—lots of people are afraid to make decisions. So don't beat yourself up, but do take steps to fix it. Top performers in any field are decisive.

Objection: "I don't like change."

- I don't think anyone loves the unknown, but embracing change is the only way to succeed.
- In business, those who resist change fall behind their competitors. The only way to see different results is to try doing different things.
- You want to help your customers, right? You have to set an example for them by leaning into change.

Here's another B2B example. Let's say you have an appointment to pitch a VP at a small business, but you know he can't make a decision without his two partners, who won't be there. You can still try to close him by putting a fence around his claim that he can't do the deal. You can empower him to feel like it's fine to take the initiative.

You might say, "John, I know you'd rather wait to make this decision until your partners get back. But you make important decisions every day, right? So how could your partners be mad at you for working with me on this great opportunity?" This plays to his sense of identity as one of the key leaders at the company.

I've found that fence staking is especially useful when pitching a "one-legger" who's afraid to talk to a rep without their spouse present. As we saw earlier in the book, a one-legger will often ask a rep to come back when the spouse will be home. But I don't want to waste my time by coming back—I want to close this deal now! I used to tell my team, "There are no comebacks." A D2D rep who can't close one-leggers will be giving up on at least 30 percent of all opportunities.

So I stake a fence around her fear: "I'm sure your husband isn't the kind of guy who'd get mad at you for taking steps to protect your home and family, right? Do you text him from Costco for permission to try a new kind of food?" These questions prime her to defend her own ability to make decisions and defend her husband as a good guy. That sets me up to get past her objection: "So you really don't need to worry about him getting mad about this, because you'll be getting a great deal on home security."

The better you become at staking fences, the less resistance you will face from customers. In fact, they will start closing themselves, which will make your job a lot more fun.

65

Rein Swapping

I GOT THE IDEA for rein swapping from a professional hypnotist who came to one of our conferences and hypnotized about thirty volunteers. I was a total skeptic and didn't think hypnosis was real . . . until this guy got me singing and dancing to a Britney Spears song, like a zombie. I wouldn't believe it if there wasn't a video.

The hypnotist taught me that there's a way to gradually take control of any conversation, the way one rider in an old-fashioned horse-drawn carriage could take over the reins that controlled the horses. I figured we could adapt that technique and teach sales reps how to subconsciously get people to do things they normally wouldn't do. It didn't have a name, so we called it rein swapping.

Imagine you and your prospect are sitting in the carriage. At first the prospect is holding the reins of the horses. They're the boss in their home or office and have all the power to steer the conversation or to bring it to a halt. Your goal is to slowly take the reins and guide the customer through the sales process. But you can't just grab the reins by force, because that's too aggressive and will turn people off.

Instead, follow a pattern that hypnotists use to subconsciously build trust, by mixing indisputable facts with leading suggestions:

Fact, fact, fact, fact.

Fact, fact, fact, LEAD.

REIN SWAP

Fact, fact, LEAD, LEAD.
Fact, LEAD, LEAD, LEAD.

The facts reassure people that you're honest and trustworthy. They subconsciously slip into a sense of security, which then makes it easier to nudge them in a direction of your choosing. Then you go back to more indisputable facts, before another leading statement. Soon you're holding the reins for most of the conversation.

But this won't work with just any facts—they have to be closely connected to the leading idea you're trying to plant. If I tell you that my shirt is green, my pants are black, and I'm a male (all indisputable facts) and then add that water tastes like honey (a leading statement), you're not going to fall for that.

On the other hand, imagine listening to this sequence while I pitch you on a new type of water bottle:

- Water is essential to human health.
- The average person's body is 60 percent water, and yours might be as much as 75 percent.
- People want to drink high-quality water, without any chlorine or gross chemicals.

- Our amazing new bottle with a built-in purifier will give you the best water you ever tasted.

That sequence was *fact, fact, fact, leading statement.* The fourth bullet is an opinion, but you may take it as a fact after hearing three facts in a row. Then I continue:

- About 95 percent of city tap water contains a significant amount of fluoride.
- There's no way to be sure what other impurities are in your tap water.
- Our bottle is the quickest and easiest way to remove all those impurities.
- It also looks cool and is easy to carry around.

That was *fact, fact, lead, lead.* I ramped up the subjective content, now that I've built up your trust with factual content. I have the reins of the conversion now, and you probably don't even realize it.

Most people want to be led, as long as they trust whoever is leading them. They don't want to feel like they have to make decisions or be in charge. They'd rather be an Uber passenger than an Uber driver. You can use this truth of psychology to gently take the reins.

As with other techniques in this section, you need to script out your lines and practice them until they sound smooth and natural. You definitely don't want to mention that you're using a principle of hypnosis! It's just a normal conversation that happens to include a lot of facts, mixed in with opinions about your product.

Rein swapping will help you sidestep objections and get back in the driver's seat, anytime you need it. Sometimes a customer will try to seize back the reins and assert dominance during the discussion. When that happens, stay calm and go back to your indisputable facts, soothing their objections and restoring their trust. Repeat as often as necessary.

66

Feel/Felt/Found (FFF)

FEEL/FELT/FOUND IS a really useful technique that I learned from Brian Tracy.

When your prospect raises a real objection, not a smoke screen, first demonstrate that you hear them and empathize with them: "I understand how you *feel*."

Then bring up an example of someone who had the same objection: "This person a lot like you *felt* the same way."

Then, good news, this other person overcame it: "Here's what they *found* . . . [solution]."

For instance, let's say your prospect objects that he needs to talk to his wife before continuing. You can use FFF like this: "I get it, it must *feel* frustrating if you can't make this kind of decision on your own. This reminds me of my customer Johnny, who *felt* the same way. But we got him set up with faster and cheaper internet anyway, and he *found* that it was totally fine with his wife. It was such a good deal for them that she had no reason to complain."

To prepare in advance for FFF, write out a kind of map. Start with a common objection, like "needs to talk to spouse." Then think of a few good stories of other customers who felt the same way but overcame the problem. If you haven't faced any of those situations personally, you can ask colleagues for some examples.

You ideally want to build up an arsenal of stories that will connect with different kinds of customers, such as men versus women, rich versus poor, and so on. The bigger your arsenal, and the more you practice telling those stories, the better you'll be able to use this technique.

67

Identify/Isolate/ Overcome (IIO)

ONE OF MY FAVORITE old sayings is "Buyers are liars." They often make stuff up to try to wiggle out of a deal. They hide their true concerns to avoid showing vulnerability. This creates problems when facing objections because it's often hard to tell what's really bothering them. To beat this kind of deception, the Identify/Isolate/Overcome (IIO) technique has three steps:

- Drill down into objections to *identify* the true source of the problem.
- Then *isolate* that problem by finding out whether it's the only concern preventing a deal, or if there are other issues too.
- Then collaborate with the prospect to *overcome* the isolated objection.

A good sign that you need to use IIO is when you hear "I would totally do this, but . . ." If whatever follows the *but* is a solvable problem, and if it truly is the only problem, you might be able to overcome it. IIO will give you that diagnosis.

For instance: "It sounds good but I need to think more about it." That's a very vague objection—what do they need to think about? I'd respond with "It feels like you still have some questions. I'm sorry that I haven't answered everything or didn't explain myself clearly. Just let me know what I can answer for you."

Then let's say the prospect replies, "I really just want to make sure this is a good price, that it's affordable."

This is getting closer to the real problem, but we're not there yet. I still need to do more identifying. "When you say *affordable*, do you mean cheap enough that you can afford it, or just that you want to make sure you're getting the best deal?"

"Just that I'm getting the best deal."

Bingo! The real problem is now identified. Now I can move on to isolating: "So if you found out that you were getting a killer deal, the best possible bang for your buck, would anything else hold you back?"

"No, but I'd like to get at least three bids from different companies. I need to compare apples to apples instead of just taking your word for it." Now the problem is both identified and isolated. If we can solve this one, we can close the deal.

"Hey, I totally understand. If I were to call our competition right now and get them to send quotes and show you the deals they're offering—and if ours is the best value—would you say yes then?"

Here I'm double-checking to make sure this is the *real* objection. If he says yes, I'd continue with something like "Awesome. I just happen to have a few examples of bids I pulled from the last few customers' homes. Those customers did the exact same comparison shopping you wanted to do." Then I'd pull the competing bids out of my backpack or pull them up on my iPad and show that we offer the best value.

(Remember: You should always pitch on *value* rather than *price*. It's not just what they're paying but the bang they're getting for their buck.)

Because this prospect has already said competitive bids are the only thing holding them back, how can they say no at this point? Assuming your value proposition really is competitive, this problem will soon be overcome.

One key to IIO is to recognize a vague objection like "I need to do more research and think about it." Vague language means there's something deeper that the prospect isn't telling you. What are they researching? What are they thinking about? A few smart questions can identify the real problem, and then you can continue from there.

68

Agree/Restate/Antidote/ Transition (ARAT)

I GOT THE Agree/Restate/Antidote/Transition (ARAT) technique from a sales mentor of mine, Kenny, back in my alarm days, and it's another powerful tool for when you hear a tough objection.

First, you want to *agree* with their concern, unless the prospect says something totally absurd. It's another way of empathizing—"I understand how you feel. I totally agree. Everyone is on a tight budget these days. Inflation is crazy."

Then you *restate* the concern back to them, but make it a lot more narrow. You modify their concern to be as isolated as possible, which is also known as pigeonholing. "I get it, no one wants to spend when the bank account is tight. But if you had enough cash on hand, you'd be all about it, right? Is the real problem the down payment, or the monthly payment too?"

Let's say you go back and forth with restating, and you find out that the real problem isn't just the initial or monthly cost, it's the total cost. "So what you're saying is that overall, the total payments are too much for your current budget. Is that right?"

Once that's clarified, you can move on to the *antidote*. You might say, "Well, I've got an idea. What if we move some stuff around in your budget? What if we could save you money on this other thing, to free up the cash you need?" Then you start to work through the problem with the customer, as teammates on the same side.

You can also drop in a story here about someone else who had a similar problem. "This situation sounds a lot like my customer Tom. What he did to free up some cash was . . ."

Then you *transition*. Remember when we covered "mind the gap" in the pitching section of the book? The same idea applies here: It's very important not to pause while waiting for the prospect's validation. You give your antidote and move on. Here's an example of how that might sound:

> *"I totally agree. Everyone is on a tight budget these days. Inflation is crazy. So what you're saying is that right now, in your current budget, you just don't have the cash. Well, we can solve that by financing this thing over twelve months. That way your monthly payment will drop to just $500 a month, and I know you can afford that. You won't have to even think about the overall price, because I'll get you a low interest rate. So I just need some basic info to get this approved. What's the best email to reach you at?"*

Did you see how this immediately transitioned into the process for setting up the financing solution? If you stop for approval first, you can easily get stuck.

Many customers will just go along with this kind of transition. But if they don't—if they say, "Whoa, I don't want to finance that!"—that's okay too. You can reply with "Oh, I thought you said you couldn't afford it up front, so you needed financing. You did say you want it, other than the cost, right?"

Now you can continue to work on the objection, by repeating the ARAT process. You might find that it takes several rounds to fully overcome it. But if you have some creative solutions in your arsenal, you can hopefully land on one that works for the customer's needs.

69

The Intentional Loop

CUSTOMER: "Sorry, I'm not interested."

Rep: "Hey, are you a big Lakers fan? I love all the swag you have here."

In a normal conversation, this exchange doesn't make any sense. But in a sales pitch, it can get you out of a major jam. It's called an intentional loop.

You can usually tell if a prospect is getting impatient or about to raise an objection, or even throw you off their doorstep or hang up. At that point you may think you need to sell even harder, to try to save the pitch from crashing.

But believe it or not, that's actually the perfect moment to *stop selling*—to switch from sales mode to human mode. Stop trying to make your pitch a straight line from A to Z, and go on a tangent. Then, when the time is right, you can loop from the tangent back into your sales process.

Here's how it works for one of the most common signs of resistance: "Sorry, this is a bad time, I'm really busy with work." That's usually an excuse, not a true objection. It gives you an opening to respond with something like "No worries, I totally understand—what do you do for work?" The prospect will probably answer that question because it's not too personal. (See Chapter 19 on the four types of questions.)

INTENTIONAL LOOP

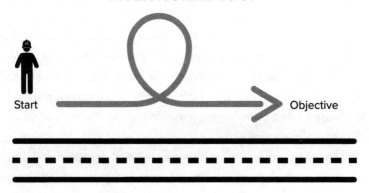

Then you can respond conversationally to whatever they say about their work. If the prospect is an engineer, what kind? What projects are they working on now? This might lead to a brief conversation about product design or quality control. Then you can loop back with a comment like "As an industrial engineer, I'm sure you can appreciate the difference between well-designed and crappy products. That's one thing I really love about my company—these HVAC systems are engineered to a very high quality standard. . . ." Now you're back in sales mode, but the prospect is more engaged than they were before you took that intentional loop.

This tactic requires improvisation, because there's no way to pregame for every potential loop. If the prospect is busy because she's a teacher grading homework, you can mention how old your kids are and see where that leads. Or if she can't talk now because she was just about to work on her garden, mention that you noticed how beautiful the garden is. How long has she been working on it? Was it already there when she moved in, or did she create it?

The intentional loop is powerful because people generally like to talk about their work or hobbies. And once they start talking to you, it's a lot easier to keep them talking. The hardest part is honing your instinct as to when's a good moment to loop back to your pitch.

I was once pitching one of my company's executive mastermind groups, the Xperts Circle, to a prospect who was acting highly skeptical. Early on, I made a mental note when he mentioned that he had just gotten back from a scuba diving trip to the Cayman Islands. When we seemed to be hitting a wall of tension, I shifted to asking, "So, do you like to travel?"

This led to a fun exchange about all the cool spots he'd been visiting recently, and how he was getting more and more into adventure travel. I listened intently and responded with interest.

When the mood was calmer and less tense, I transitioned back to my pitch. "The best part about our CEO mastermind group is that we do an international trip once a year, with epic adventures in awesome places. It's the coolest way to mastermind and network with other high-level people. Our next trip is happening next month. Let's get you on board so you can be part of the fun!"

We ended up closing the deal—a $30,000 per year commitment for five years as part of that mastermind group. And he wound up becoming a real friend along the way. But it never would have happened without the intentional loop.

PART EIGHT

Closing

70

Introduction to Closing

I BET SOME OF YOU have flipped ahead to this section of the book without reading the rest. Whenever I talk about sales, people want to jump ahead to closing. It's a popular subject because it's fun. It's the moment when you actually make money and get to celebrate with an end zone dance. It's when you get the biggest dopamine rush.

But many reps don't realize that the key groundwork for closing starts long before the actual close. If you neglect to build the right foundation during your presentation, you will probably face high resistance when you ask for the sale. Everything you've been learning and practicing up until now is essential before you try to master the tactics in this section.

On the other hand, if you're great at prospecting, pitching, and presenting, but you suck at closing, none of that preliminary stuff will maximize your potential. You'll end up with a bunch of noncommittal maybes and a lot of frustration. So let's get you better at closing!

In this section I'll give you the guiding principles of closing and some key tactics you can practice and add to your arsenal. Those will be enough to help you become a very good closer. Then if you want even more detail about even more closing scenarios, I recommend that you pick up another book of mine, called *The ABC's of Closing*.

71

The Yes Train

THE YES TRAIN IS a simple concept, but it might be the single most powerful closing skill you need to master.

A lot of salespeople get in trouble because they're constantly pushing, pushing, pushing toward a close. Every element of their pitch and presentation is high pressure, and the prospect may feel like they're being nudged toward a cliff. Then at the climactic moment, when they reach the edge of the cliff, they look down and feel terrified. Who wants to take a leap of faith into an empty void?

The Yes Train avoids forcing your prospect into one big decision of buying versus not buying—so they will never feel like they got pushed off the cliff and are hurtling toward the ground. Instead, imagine a train making a series of gentle switchbacks as it gradually zigzags downward, from the top of the cliff to the ground below. That's a much more appealing way to get down to the ground, isn't it? In fact, if the train makes enough gradual loops, it will hardly feel like it's descending.

This means that you should aim to create a series of micro-closes that aren't scary at all. Each one will get the prospect to agree to something that feels safe, such as a statement about their needs, wishes, and budget. The combined impact of these micro-closes will lead the prospect gently and naturally to the conclusion that they should buy your offering.

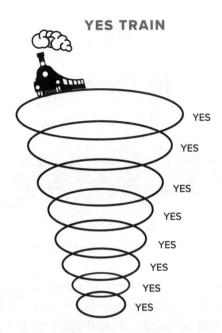

YES TRAIN

YES

YES

YES

YES

YES

YES

YES

YES

Depending on the situation, you might have twenty, thirty, or even fifty micro-closes built into your entire interaction, from first contact to final signature on a contract. As Brian Tracy says, "Closing is anything that gets you closer to a sale."

If you look back through this book, you'll see that a lot of our tactics at each stage are actually setting up micro-closes. For instance, remember "Be the needed, not the needy"? That attitude signals low pressure and low stress. It's one of many steps telling the prospect that there's no need to be afraid, because you aren't going to throw them off a cliff.

So as we go through various closing tactics in this part of the book, keep in mind that closing really starts long before you get to the literal stage of closing. If you've been mixing in micro-closes from the beginning, heading into the homestretch will feel a lot smoother and easier—for both you and your customer.

72

Tie-Downs

TIE-DOWNS ARE CLOSELY RELATED to the Yes Train. They're another way to turn closing from a single huge step into a series of smaller, much less scary steps.

The idea came to me when I was watching the Jack Black movie *Gulliver's Travels*, based on Jonathan Swift's 1726 novel (which I've never read but assume isn't as fun as the Jack Black version). Poor Gulliver ends up in a strange land called Lilliput, where the tiny residents think he's a terrifying giant. To capture him, they tie Gulliver down with a whole bunch of little strings. Any one of those strings would be easy for him to break, but when they add one string after another, after another, after another, he's stuck.

As a metaphor for closing, the little strings are simple questions you can ask customers that lead to small commitments over the course of your entire interaction. Eventually you will build up enough small commitments that the customer is tied down into completing the closing. Their own answers have already done most of the work, before you even get to the actual closing stage.

Some examples of Tie-Down questions that you can drop into your pitch or presentation, and where they might lead:

"What do you love the most about our product so far?"

Let's say they reply, "I really love how you can control it with your phone." That's great, because now they're on the record as liking your product. It will be hard for them to backtrack later and claim they aren't interested. No one wants to be caught in an obvious lie.

"Would you be most likely to get this because you think it's a good deal, or you like the way it feels, or both?"

If they say, "Good deal," you now simply have to prove that you're offering a good deal. If they say, "The way it feels," you now have to get them to acknowledge that your product feels great. Either of those steps should be manageable if you have the right facts handy.

When I used to sell alarm systems, I found that a sequence of three questions became a really powerful Tie-Down that led to many successful closes. I made sure all three were built into my presentation and never skipped them:

First: "Are you the kind of person who tells other people about products or services you like?" If they said yes, I'd continue: "That's cool, because we love to work with people who give referrals. We can get you a bigger discount and a referral bonus if you help us out that way." This helps reinforce that we're on the same team.

Second: "When do you think you'd mainly use the alarm system? When you go out and no one's home, or mainly at night when you're asleep, to protect your family?" This was a trick question—most people use an alarm system for both. Once they replied that they'd probably do both, I'd follow up: "Great, do you think you'd probably use it every day, or once a week, or once a month?" Now I'd usually have them on the record that they'd use the alarm system for both purposes every day. That was a strong combination of tie-down strings!

Third: "What would be the main reason that would persuade you to sign up for our system? Would it be the ease of use, the peace of mind, or competitive pricing?" No matter what they answer, it's another sign that they want to buy. Which I would definitely remind them of later.

Taking the time to build questions like these into your presentation is super powerful. It's starting your close before you actually get to your close. So think about what kinds of questions you can ask to get your customers to tie themselves down. The key is to make the questions sound very casual, no big deal. For instance:

- Would it be cool if we put the unit right here, or do you have another spot in mind?
- Would you guys want the app on multiple phones or just on one phone?
- How many users would you want to get licenses for our software?

Salespeople often talk about closing as a complex process. But as you learn more and more closing techniques, don't forget the power of asking simple questions. They can bring your customers closer and closer to tying themselves down.

73

The ABC's of Closing

I'M SURE YOU'VE HEARD the old saying "Never bring a knife to a gunfight." My approach to closing is to bring a knife *and* a gun—plus a flamethrower, a rocket launcher, and some grenades. You never know what you might be up against! The more strategies you add to your arsenal, the more prepared you'll be for unexpected situations. And if one type of closing starts to hit a brick wall, you can switch to another.

With that in mind, here's a summary of twenty-six approaches to closing that I explored in one of my previous books, *The ABC's of Closing.* If you want the full details on all twenty-six, plus some additional bonus closes, I encourage you to read it. Closing is worth as much studying and practicing as you can devote to it.

A: The Assumption Close

This means assuming the customer will say yes and stating future steps as if they're inevitable. Suppose I'm selling new window replacements and I say, "Your new windows are going to stay cleaner much longer because we use a special type of glass that repels dirt."

By acting as if the customer has already said yes, and using a matter-of-fact tone, you signal that saying yes is the most natural thing in the world. Calling them "your new windows" instead of "our windows" creates a sense of assumption and ownership. It's similar to the psychology of Tie-Downs and the Yes Train.

B: The Bandwagon Close

We talked about bandwagoning as part of prospecting, and sometimes you'll want to bring it back for closing. It's simply dropping the names of other customers your prospect might know, to build a sense of peer pressure. If other people are solving their pain points with your solution, the prospect will probably want to do likewise. You need to do advance research to make sure you're quoting appropriate doppelgängers, ideally those who have agreed to serve as references.

"Hey, the Jones family down the street got this same package, and they're really happy with it."

"I worked with another plumbing company in the next town over, Richardson Plumbing. Do you know those guys? They love our software."

C: The Competition Close

Telling your customer about a competition can be surprisingly effective, if they're on the fence. Companies often create sales competitions to motivate their reps. If you share what you're competing for, and why, you can trigger some empathy and an authentic desire to help you reach your goal. You can also create a sense of urgency for a customer who might be prone to delaying. For instance:

"We're in the last few days of our competition and I'm just behind the leader."

"I would be letting my whole team down if you say no."

"My wife is really counting on me to win that trip to Hawaii."

You might be reluctant to share your personal goals this way, but self-disclosure can make you seem more like a real human being, not just another sleazy salesperson. You can even show pictures of your spouse or kids to reinforce why you're working so hard to win this sales competition.

D: The Discount Close

People instinctively love a limited-time deal, such as "20 percent off during Memorial Day weekend." Knowing that they got a discount helps them feel better about buying now rather than waiting to do more research. You want to convince them that this deal will give the biggest bang for their buck. A deal for less money is better than no deal at all—especially if you can get referrals to other high-quality leads in return.

But be careful not to get into a habit of overdoing it on discounts. That's the lazy way of closing; it will make you weak, and in the long term you'll sell less. Make sure that any discount you offer won't eat too much into your commission or the company's profit. Remind yourself that you're selling a good product for a fair price, and there's no need to give away the store. You also have to stick to your word. If you say that a discount is valid only if they say yes today, don't offer it again tomorrow!

E: The Excuses Close

This builds on the difference between a smoke screen and a true objection. People often make excuses for not buying that turn out to be just smoke, if you probe them with a few smart questions. You then want to flip their excuse into the *reason* to buy.

If you hear a likely excuse such as "I can't afford it," be prepared with a good comeback:

"That's exactly why this makes sense! Most people don't want to spend the money, until they see how much it will cost them to say no. Over time this will save you countless hours of work. In fact, adding up all that time, you actually can't afford *not* to do this."

People often turn to an excuse when they don't feel compelled to decide right now. So you really have two missions. First, give them emotionally compelling reasons to be enthusiastic. Second, show that their excuse, whatever it is, really isn't enough to hold them back.

F: The Feel/Felt/Found Close

We covered this in the objections section, and it works very powerfully when added to any kind of close. It has the advantage of using a third party to validate your response to an objection. Remember the three-part structure:

"I understand how you *feel*. So-and-so *felt* the same way because. . . . But then they *found* that our product worked great for them, because . . ."

The "found" part can be as long or short as you want to make it. If you have a great story about another customer who had the same objection and found that it didn't matter, tell it. Then you can simply ask if the customer is ready to move forward, now that you've hopefully eased their fears.

G: The Give-and-Take Close

Some customers will try to take advantage of you by extracting one concession after another. Maybe a lower price, a free month, a waived activation fee, anything like that. You might be so eager to close that you're willing to give and give and give, until you've given away the store. That's a terrible situation for you.

When you encounter a customer who loves to negotiate for special favors, turn it into a give-and-take relationship. For instance: "If I get you the extra hundred-dollar discount you're asking for, I'm going to need a favor in return. Can you give me referrals to three friends who might also be really good customers? That would be a fair trade, right?"

Now you're back in charge, instead of just reacting to their demands. You don't necessarily need to ask for referrals; you can ask for a signature today instead of next week, or a five-star online review, or even just a glass of water and a banana on a hot day. What matters is establishing the give-and-take, to signal that you won't be walked all over. Once you've got this kind of win-win deal, the rest of the close should go smoothly.

H: The High-Five Close

This one might sound silly, but it's grounded in psychology. State a point that you know your customer will agree with, then follow up with a high five. That moment of interpersonal touch takes your connection to a new level. The same is true for a fist bump or a friendly pat on the shoulder, if one of those feels appropriate.

A high five is less formal and business coded than a handshake. Friends and teammates give each other high fives, so you're signaling that you're definitely on the customer's side. Even if they're trying to stay serious and professional during your pitch, a high five subconsciously makes them see you as a friend. And then you'll be one step closer to closing.

It's extremely rare for a customer to leave you hanging when you try a high five. We've all been conditioned since childhood to return them. So even if the customer isn't fully on board yet, the high five will loosen them up a little and make them smile.

I: The Intelligence Close

The intelligence close is similar to the bandwagon close, but you're appealing to respected, intelligent experts instead of regular people who match the customer's profile. We covered some examples earlier in the book. Depending on what you're selling, you might tell a story about how doctors and engineers love your product. Or you might name-drop celebrity endorsers like Kim Kardashian or Shaquille O'Neal, if they actually use it.

On the other hand, if you're selling financial planning for small business owners, your customers probably *won't* be impressed to hear that Kim or Shaq uses your services. They want to hear that successful business owners endorse you. A guy who nets $100,000 a year wants to know who the folks who net $1 million trust with their money. It doesn't matter if the examples you talk about aren't famous, as long as they match your customers' idea of an intelligent role model—one more successful and therefore probably smarter than they are.

J: The "Just Do It" Close

Some customers need a little burst of confidence to stop waffling and second-guessing their own impulse to say yes. In these situations, simply saying something like "Just do it" can pull them over the finish line.

At a moment like that, stop going into the weeds about your offering and cut to the chase: "John, we've been talking about this for a while and I know you really want it. The product is a good fit for you. The price is a good deal. You like it, and you like me. Let's just do it!"

You can also give an example of someone else who took the plunge: "The Johnsons down the street were tight on money, and they weren't 100 percent sure this was the right fit, but they trusted me and they *just did it.* Now they're thrilled with the product and the great deal they got."

K: The "Knocked on Your Door" Close

Sometimes you need to remind customers that you intentionally came to them, so it's not like they wandered into a store. You wouldn't be wasting your time, or theirs, if you hadn't done advance research to know they're a good fit. For instance: "I knocked on your door to earn your business, so I know I have to make it worth your while just to hear me out. I respect your time, and I'm asking you respectfully to give me some of yours, because this will make sense."

You can leverage the fact that sales is a tough job and play on the customer's empathy. If you sell D2D, you might mention that you've been walking around for two hours and have two more hours to go until you can take a break. That's another way to let the customer into your world, so you'll seem more human.

But be careful not to go too far and slide into neediness. Remember: "Be the needed, not the needy." Remember your abundance mindset: you aren't desperate, because you have plenty of business. This will help you show as much respect for yourself as you show to the customer. No one trusts a desperate salesperson who seems like they'd say or do anything to close a sale. That's not you!

L: The "Last Chance" Close

You can create a genuine, positive sense of urgency by giving the customer one last chance to buy, before the price or offering will change. Urgency is valuable, because if you don't close on your first contact, the likelihood of ever closing drops tremendously. But there's an art to creating urgency without crossing the line into obnoxious pushiness. For instance:

"My boss told me that the first five people I sign in your town will get a super-deep promotional rate so we can generate referrals for future business. I've already signed up four, so this is your last chance to grab this special opportunity."

"Today only, we're waiving the installation fee as an incentive to boost our numbers by the end of the month. So if you're interested you should really grab this offer today, or else you'll have to pay an extra $400 for installation."

"You're very lucky that our techs are only three blocks away, working on someone else's house. If we can wrap up the paperwork now, I can get the $400 installation fee waived because they're already in town. You'll also avoid the usual waiting period. But if you wait to decide after today, you'll have to pay for installation."

This close is most effective if you use it before any major objections come up. It isn't helpful to backpedal and introduce urgency after they've already told you they don't want to buy today.

M: The Manager Call Close

When a customer is asking for a better deal, you can make them feel special by needing to ask approval from your manager. Then when you succeed in winning that approval, they'll feel grateful that you're on their side, and thus they will be more likely to buy.

Before you call, you need to make it clear that you're going above and beyond what you'd normally do. Some examples:

"Hypothetically, if I call my manager and get him to approve knocking ten dollars off the monthly fee, would you do it?"

"I can't do any better on the price without my manager's approval.

But he hates it if I call him too often. Before I ask him for a favor to help you, I just want to make sure I'm not wasting one of my calls."

"I can't make any promises, but maybe I can get my manager to approve an extra 10 percent discount. He hates doing that and usually yells at me when I ask. But if you're telling me the rest of this process will go smoothly if I can convince him, I'll give it my best shot."

N: The "Not Interested" Close

As we've discussed, when a customer flat out says they're "not interested," that's probably an excuse rather than a real objection. It may mean they just don't feel like processing what you're saying. You can poke holes in the excuse by pointing out that "not interested" is different from not needing or wanting. You can also go back to the 8-Mile technique, to head off other possible objections. For instance:

"Most people I meet aren't super interested in X until after they need it. But once they need it, it's too late. We take more of a proactive approach. I'm here to help you be prepared in advance."

"I get it. This isn't a fun thing to buy, and it hasn't been at the top of your interest list. Most people are the same way, because they focus on what they're interested in rather than what they need. I'm here to help you stop procrastinating and get this done, the cheapest and easiest way possible."

"I bet a lot of other sales guys have been coming to your door about this, right? I hate when that happens. I bet that's why you're saying you're not interested, right? Perfect, because I'm doing something totally different. . . ."

O: The Option Close

This strategy plays on the human desire to be in control and make decisions. You give your customer two (or at the most three) options to choose the next step. You're fine with any of these options, so what you're really doing is converting a yes-or-no decision into a yes-or-yes decision. Our brains can process only so many bits per second, so if you narrow things down to just a couple of choices, you'll make the decision much easier.

Some examples:

"Do you prefer ten-year or fifteen-year financing?

"Do you prefer the lowest monthly payment or the overall lowest total cost?"

"We can install it on Tuesday. What's easiest for you—noon, three p.m., or six p.m.?"

"Are you more interested in the premium package or the basic package?"

If you get a straight answer to your options question, awesome. But if you get pushback or a refusal to choose, you may need to pull back to spark more interest or build more trust. Ask deeper questions and spend more time in discovery before offering another option to proceed.

P: The Puppy Dog Close

Sometimes the way to get a customer to say yes is to offer a trial period with easy cancellation. This close gets its name from pet stores and dog shelters, because when people take a puppy home for a trial run before adopting, they usually fall in love with it. A trial period makes it extremely hard to walk away.

On the downside, if your customer doesn't love your product as much as a cute puppy, you'll have to deal with the hassle of cancellation. But that risk can be worth it for the chance to close a sale today that will *probably* stick. Try something like:

> "You have nothing to lose by trying it out. You have three business days to cancel and get 100 percent of your money back, guaranteed."

> "Would you ever buy a car without test-driving it? This is the same kind of situation. I recommend that you give it a spin for a couple of days. If you don't like it, we can come back and it won't cost you a dime."

> "We're so confident in the value this will generate, we're giving you the first month free. If it doesn't knock your socks off in that first month, you can easily cancel."

Q: The Qualifying Close

Remember early in the book when we talked about qualifying your prospects? You might want to revisit qualifying when you're about to close. Pull back by showing uncertainty about whether or not the customer is even eligible for your deal. This reinforces that you aren't desperate—that you're the needed, not the needy. It can get them in the mindset of hoping they *can* buy, instead of wondering if they *should* buy.

You can ask about various qualifying factors depending on what you're selling, but a good one is credit rating. "How's your credit?" is a simple question that most people can easily answer. People with high credit scores are usually proud of it. You can make them feel even better by saying something like "That's great, because my company is really picky about credit ratings. We have to turn away a lot of customers who don't qualify for financing. But you won't have any problem."

I like to make a big deal of the fact that a customer meets our tough standards. They're special, and now they can move forward with this awesome deal. Yay! How can they possibly say no after you've already celebrated?

R: The Research Close

Some customers try to stall a decision by saying they need to do more research. You can head off this objection by doing the research for them. This can reassure them that they aren't getting suckered; you really do have a great offering at a fair price.

Realistically, almost no one wants to sit at a computer for hours, googling your competitors and reading every piece of information available about your product or service. They don't want to call half a dozen other companies for price quotes. If you leave without closing, they may have every intention of doing more research, but it's more likely that your business card will be tossed aside and forgotten.

You can start by saying you're happy to spend as much time as they need getting answers to their questions. And in fact you've got a bunch of detailed research, if they'd like to see it. You can show them reputable information instead of whatever random opinions they might find on the web.

Then add something like "If you had proof that you were getting a great deal on a great product, and that our company is legit, would you do it?" Then guide them through the research you brought, and lock them down!

S: The Spouse Close

Earlier in the book we covered the challenge of selling to someone who won't make a decision without their spouse. Another way to think about spouses is in terms of getting one of them to help you close the other. If both are physically at home during a D2D sale, but only one is listening, do everything possible to get the other one in front of you at the same time. You'll take away the common excuse that no decision can be made without discussing it with the spouse.

The same is true for business partners in a B2B selling scenario. If you get an appointment to pitch a small business, try to get all the partners in the room at the same time.

Most married couples—and business partnerships—have one person who serves as the primary decision-maker. Never assume who that is or rely on gender stereotypes. You can screw up your entire sale by focusing on the wrong person and neglecting the one with veto power. You can usually tell if both are present, because the one with less power will look to the decision-maker for validation. The decision-maker tends to speak up more quickly and is usually tougher to persuade.

Whether you have both spouses in front of you or just the junior partner, your job is to make the junior partner your ally in convincing the decision-maker. Use all the techniques you've learned in this book to build rapport and trust. Then establish your partnership with them by saying something like "Hey, you have to help me work on your wife. Please tell her all the reasons why this would be so good for your family." If the decision-maker isn't there, you can suggest calling them together to avoid the much worse option of coming back another time.

T: The Time Frame Close

Setting expectations on your time frame is another way to create urgency and ease the customer's anxiety. They may not realize that a sales process typically takes just one visit, and they will be expected to make a decision today. You can set up for a close by clearly explaining that this won't be a drawn-out, back-and-forth process. This message works well when coupled with the Knocked on Your Door close.

No one likes surprises. By setting clear expectations for the time frame, you can alleviate the customer's fear of the unknown while putting yourself in control of the situation. After you walk your customer through the basic steps to come, you'll find that most simply follow those steps to a decision point. Make sure you include how long each step will take so your customer won't worry that you might bend their ear for the next three hours. For instance:

> "It will take about twenty minutes to go over our program, maybe a little more if you have a lot of questions. Then if you're happy with everything, I can put the paperwork through today. Then the installation usually happens within a week."

> "You can set the timer on your phone for twenty minutes. If I'm not done by then, or if you're not 100 percent sold on this when the timer goes off, I'll leave and stop bugging you. Does that sound fair?"

U: The Upsell Price Drop Close

We all see prices as relative, not absolute. Is a $500 television expensive? It depends on whether the similar ones next to it at Best Buy cost $750 to $1,000 or $200 to $400. You can take advantage of this by first upselling your customer on a very expensive option and then dropping the price to a more modest option that fits their actual needs.

You never know who might buy your most expensive offering or package, which is reason enough to include it as an option in every presentation. But more important, it's much easier to start with a high-priced package and then come down, rather than starting with a basic package and trying to add onto it. Customers always feel better when they see prices coming down.

My favorite example is Cutco knives. They offer a super-deluxe knife set that costs around $3,000. Very few people buy it, but it makes Cutco's $300 and $200 sets look very affordable.

V: The Virgin Territory Close

If your company is new, or new to a particular area, your potential customers probably won't have heard of you or seen any of your advertising. That sounds like a big disadvantage, but you can flip it around to a plus by using the Virgin Territory close.

You explain that, unlike the big guys, your company doesn't waste millions on advertising. Instead you're investing in creating a great offering at a great price. You might say something like:

> "We are fairly new to the area. To get the word of mouth rolling, we're giving our first twenty customers a 20 percent discount. This is a onetime only opportunity, and all we ask in return is some suggestions of other families in town who might also be interested."

> "Because we're new, we're looking for a few people who qualify for our initial program, to get the ball rolling in your neighborhood. There are a few qualifications you'd have to meet, but we'll give you free installation and a free first month of service. No other company in town is doing that."

W: The Why Close

This is a type of Tie-Down, and as we covered in Chapter 72, Tie-Downs are a great way to get someone primed to buy. You ask the customer to list the reasons why they like your product or service. You might need to prompt them with a few suggestions to jump-start their list, such as price or convenience. But ideally the customer will come up with as many whys as they can think of. The simple act of listing them will create a powerful urge to say yes.

The best time to use this close is right before you get into pricing. Once the customer is feeling passionate about the reasons they want to buy, it will be harder for them to push back on whatever the price is.

X: The X Marks the Spot Close

It may sound silly, but you can help your customer get through an intimidating contract or other paperwork by showing them exactly where to initial or sign. Otherwise the legalese might create some last-minute jitters about taking the final step. As you go through a contract, explain what each signature or initial signifies, such as "This part is your consent for us to do the installation. . . . This part is where you acknowledge that I explained the three-day cancellation policy."

If you want to make the paperwork even easier for them, you can fill out as much as possible yourself. For example, every alarm company needs an emergency contact in case the alarm goes off and the homeowner doesn't answer their phone. I would ask the customer to tell me the name and number they wanted me to write so they wouldn't be stuck holding the pen while they pondered the question.

Do you remember when we covered the three kinds of tones in Chapter 25? At the signature stage, it really helps if you use a down tone to signal confidence. When you say, "Sign here," it should imply a command rather than a question. Not in a bossy way, just very matter-of-fact.

Y: The Yes, Yes, Yes Close

This is another name for the Yes Train, which we've already covered. A series of small yes answers lead the customer smoothly to the bigger yes. The more positive responses you add to your train, the more momentum you'll have going to the finish line.

Z: The Zero-Down Close

This means offering a special deal with no cost up front. This strategy won't always be possible, but it can be powerful to tell the customer that no payment is required at the time of sale. It's another quirk of psychology: money spent today feels more real than money committed to be spent tomorrow. So if you can make a commitment painless today, you'll remove a potential source of resistance. Don't be afraid to talk about financing options.

Sometimes it's even worth giving up a little commission to cover their first payment, if that's what it takes to close. Obviously you can't do that all the time, or you'll seriously hurt your income. But try it a few times and see what happens. I would put this in the category of a last-ditch close, if you sense that the only real obstacle is the initial expense. You want the customer to feel as if they'd be making a big mistake to walk away, because your offering is so stinking good. For instance:

> "Normally we require an initial payment of X, but I really want to help you out. If we can get this done today, I'll take care of all your up-front costs. Your first payment won't be due for a full month. Can we call that a deal?"

Building Up Your Arsenal

Again, I encourage you to pick up a copy of *The ABC's of Closing* for more details on all of these strategies, plus even more bonus closes. You can practice them with a friend in a role-playing scenario.

If this seems like an intimidating amount of material, don't be alarmed. You don't have to master all of these closes to be a great salesperson! Just pick a few to start, whichever ones sound most helpful to your specific situation. Then try mixing and matching them into your actual sales process, and take notes on what is or isn't working. Everyone's ranking of the power of these closes may be a little different.

Your ultimate goal is to gradually build up an arsenal of closing skills, then keep adding to it. Before too long, you will become a master of the art of closing.

74

Getting Referrals after the Close

HAVE YOU LOVED THIS BOOK? What three takeaways are you most eager to apply to your sales process? Considering what you paid for the book, how much value do you think you're going to get in extra commissions? Do you think there are other people in your circle who could definitely benefit from reading it? So can you please text a link to buy it to three of them right now?

Even after you have a signed deal, you're still not done. Even if you're exhausted, or feel like you can't bring up one more issue, or don't want to risk upsetting your customer, you still need to bring up referrals. They are a fundamental part of the closing process, and they can turbocharge your overall results.

Referrals are one of the big differences between carnivores and herbivores. A carnivore is constantly thinking about ways to turn one sale into five extra leads, while an herbivore is waiting for someone else to provide leads. Hunting for referrals is a low-cost, time-efficient way to multiply your success and put you far ahead of your competition.

Even better, leads that come from satisfied customers' referrals are the highest-quality leads of all, with the highest probability of closing.

They even have the secondary value of reinforcing your bond with your new customer. If they're willing to give you the names and numbers of friends, they are truly on your side now. That means they're more likely to stick with you for the long run, and maybe buy from you again if the opportunity arises.

So don't feel embarrassed about asking for referrals. People who feel like they got a good deal will be willing to share their satisfaction with friends. It's an act of generosity, like telling a friend about an awesome new restaurant. It feels good to the referrer—so why would you want to deprive them of that opportunity to feel good?

I developed a ten-step referral system that usually takes about ten minutes. Depending on your offering, you can do it immediately after your close, or later on after the customer has taken delivery. The exact timing matters less than making sure you do these steps after every close, without fail.

Step 1: Start with a Pre-Frame

The pre-frame opens the subject of referrals during a contract signing, or during a follow-up call or visit. You thank the customer again for their business, then say something like "I just want to go over one last thing that's very important, because it's how I get most of my business. Can we take a few minutes to brainstorm if anyone you know might also be a good fit? We have a special referral program that can get you a bonus if any of your referrals work out."

Step 2: Give Positive Feedback

Now you want to put them in a state of appreciation for the sales experience they went through, whether it just happened or it ended a week or a month earlier. Thank them sincerely for being a great customer and a pleasure to work with. Then ask a few questions to surface their memories of why they decided to buy and the value they've gotten so far. If they don't remember those positive feelings, they probably won't want to give you referrals.

You might ask something like "If you were to tell somebody about our product, what's the one thing you'd be most enthusiastic about?" Hopefully that will get them talking about benefits X and Y that really appealed to them. Here are other questions that should trigger positive feedback:

- "What did you like most about our conversation?"
- "Do you feel like I took care of you and answered all of your questions?"
- "What did you like most about the product or service?"

Step 3: Ask for Help

A lot of salespeople are reluctant to admit they need help, but most customers feel good about helping someone if it can be done with minimal time and effort. This is especially true if you've disclosed something personal, like maybe you're expecting your first child soon, or you're trying to save money to support an elderly parent.

After you thank the customer for their feedback, add a simple request: "Would you mind helping me out with something that's super important to me?"

Step 4: Share a Specific Goal

You'll get more referrals if you're very specific about why they matter to you, beyond just making more money. The customer will feel a stronger bond with you and will develop an interest in your success. Here's one example:

> "Right now I'm just slightly behind the best rep in the company, and it would mean a ton if I could knock him out of first place. Whoever comes out on top this quarter will win a new snow-

board, and I really love snowboarding! There's only a few days to go. So if you could refer me to some of your friends and family who'd be a good fit, that would mean the world to me."

You can also talk about a more serious goal, like how you're trying to save enough to buy a home before your first child is due in a few months. Or maybe that you really need to boost your numbers because your boss has been riding your butt lately, and you're worried about your job security.

Step 5: Share Your Ideal Client Profile

This step reinforces that you don't want referrals to just anyone. You have a few key characteristics, no more than five, that identify people who are the best fit. The more specific you can be, the more referrals your customer will probably think of—even though you probably assume the opposite, that you should cast a wide net. Here are some typical filters:

- We only want homeowners.
- We only want folks who will appreciate cutting their electric bills.
- We only want people who are nice enough to hear me out.

Step 6: Brainstorm People Who Fit

Now you can ask the customer to look through their phone. They can quickly flip through recent calls, texts, Facebook notifications, or Instagram DMs. While they do that, you can ask the customer some simple thought joggers to help them narrow down all those names:

- Anyone in your neighborhood?
- People you went to high school with?
- Folks you see at church?
- Anyone with kids under five?
- How about your old college friends?

As they start to name names, give positive feedback to encourage the customer to keep going:

- Great, he sounds perfect!
- Thanks so much, I bet they're going to love it!
- That's a good one, I bet she'll be grateful to hear about this.

Step 7: Ask for Introductions

It's one thing to end up with a list of names and numbers, but it's *much* better to have your customer introduce you to their friends and family directly. The best way they can do that is with a three-way text or email. You can text the customer a simple message template that they can quickly copy and paste. It might sound like this:

> *"Hey [name], I'm connecting you with Sam Taggart, our rep for the alarm system we bought a few weeks ago. We love it and Sam's a great guy, so I thought you might want to chat with him. No pressure, he's super easy to work with!"*

In some cases your customer might even make a call, which could be even better. If she mentions her sister, for instance, ask if she can try calling her now and pass you the phone. If that call goes to voicemail, no worries, you can still do a text intro. But if you end up talking to the sister, you might be able to pitch her the same day or the next day.

Step 8: Thank the Customer

This should be obvious, but it's easy to forget to thank the customer during the excitement of gathering referrals. Make sure you give sincere appreciation for how much they're trusting you. If they recommend you to people they care about but you then burn them, you'd be making your customer look terrible! So every referral is an act of vulnerability. You want them to feel good about taking this chance on you.

Try something like "Thank you so much for helping me out. You're an amazing connector. Even if none of these people end up buying from me, I'm going to take really good care of them and give them my best professional advice. Best-case scenario, they'll love it and you'll get a referral bonus. I'll keep you updated!"

Step 9: Follow Up

This one should also be obvious, but you'd be amazed how many salespeople blow it. Make sure you actually follow up promptly with each referral! If the customer got vulnerable and trusted you with leads to their friends, ignoring them would basically be a slap in the face. You're not just making yourself look bad; you're making your customer look bad.

If you can't send those texts or emails immediately, you have to do them within twenty-four hours of the referral. Don't embarrass yourself or your customer, even if you have to force yourself at the end of a busy day.

Step 10: Give Feedback

Finally, give your customer feedback on how the referrals are going. It doesn't have to be fancy, just a simple text or email: "Hey, thanks again for those referrals. Tom was super nice but he already has an alarm system. I'm meeting with Jennifer tomorrow evening. And best of all, Steve is on board! That's a $100 bonus coming your way! Who else have you got?"

This reinforces that you keep your word and you respect the customer. And it can easily lead to even more referrals.

I CALL THIS REFERRAL STRATEGY *leapfrogging*, because it's possible to leap from customer to customer like a frog jumping on lily pads. It will compound your results while requiring you to do much less cold-calling or cold knocking. Cultivating referrals can be fast, cheap, and super effective, leading to a lot more deals and commissions. It's the best possible use of your time.

PART
NINE

The Big
Picture

75

Managing Your Career

AS YOU GET BETTER and better at selling like a carnivore, your skills will be in high demand. This will give you lots of options for where you choose to work, and what you will and won't tolerate from employers. I strongly suggest making your career choices not purely based on money, but also on other factors.

You first want to consider how you feel about the product or service you're representing. Do you feel good about it, or are you selling something with a dark side that's slowly grinding down your self-perception as a good person? I know some people who think like hired guns and would sell anything, maybe including nukes for terrorists. That's not me, and I hope it's not you either.

Then there are quality of life factors, including how a company or manager treats you. If you're getting yelled at every day even when your results are good, why should you put up with that? A carnivore can make just as much or even more money without tolerating insults or abuse. Go find a workplace that respects you.

Another big factor should be the level of your colleagues. It might be tempting to stay with a mediocre sales force so you can consistently dominate the leaderboard. But if you can beat the field with ease, you may be tempted to hang back and coast. In the long run, you're better off in the middle of the pack at a really elite sales force.

Competing with other reps who match or exceed your skills will inspire you to keep elevating your game.

For instance, if you work at a mediocre car dealership where everybody's sitting around drinking coffee and shooting the bull, and the end of every month is a mad scramble to make quota, that's bad for your career! Find a better dealership where people are motivated by excellence and healthy competition, not just scratching out a living from month to month.

You can think of it like real estate. Do you want to buy the most expensive house in a crappy neighborhood, or the cheapest house in a really nice neighborhood? You want the cheap house on the nice street, because the rising values all around you will make your house appreciate too. That's way more important than feeling like the big shot on your block.

As a team leader and now as a CEO, my mantra is "Either change the team or change the team." If the group you manage is stagnant and mediocre, either motivate them to get better or find some new people who are willing to do the work.

The same is true for an individual making career decisions. If it looks like your team is stuck or moving in reverse, it's probably time to move. Never stick with a team that's dragging you down, even if the short-term money seems great.

I told you about that first summer I sold D2D for Platinum Protection in 2008. After that I took two years off to go on a mission for my church. When I returned to Platinum in 2011, I hit the ground running again, becoming the number-eight top-selling rep out of about four hundred. But I noticed that the culture had changed for the worse in the two years I was away. A lot of the best people had quit, and the old vibe of high achievement was now missing. It felt like a slowly sinking ship.

So I interviewed with some other alarm companies, including Vivint. Their hiring manager explained that my one hundred sixty-eight closed deals at Platinum, which was enough to make me number eight there, would have put me much lower down at Vivint. They had a smaller force in that office, about one hundred reps, but they were averaging one hundred new accounts per rep. Their top-tier reps were closing more than two hundred.

Platinum pleaded with me to stay and offered me the best pay scale they could possibly afford. But my gut told me to turn it down and go with the culture of excellence at Vivint. "Changing the team" turned out to be one of the best career moves I ever made. Over the next few years, Vivint gave me great opportunities to build and lead my own team, vastly expanding my skill set. That set me up for my future roles as a sales VP and later as CEO of my own company.

Meanwhile, Platinum kept losing talented people, because carnivores always have options. Before long Platinum lost their funding and went out of business.

My personal results jumped in my new environment, almost doubling in a single year from one hundred sixty-eight deals to about three hundred. That was enough to make me the eighth best rep in all of Vivint nationwide. A friend who made the same jump from Platinum to Vivint went from about one hundred to more than two hundred deals. We were all cranking in a high-performance culture with healthy internal competition. The following year, five out of the forty reps in our office (including me) closed more than two hundred new accounts each.

A few years later, I was working as the VP of direct sales for Clear Solar in Utah. I was beaming with energy, excited to crush it, and my mission was to rocket launch them to the top of the solar industry. If anything, I was too ambitious at that point—my personal life and my marriage became collateral damage to my workaholism. But I was able to grow the sales team from five to eighty reps within a month, and we started rocking with far better results.

Then, without warning, the top management put on a hiring freeze.

Alarm bells went off in my head. What kind of direct sales company puts a freeze on hiring, with a commission model where there's almost no risk in growing the sales force? I tried to let it slide, but my entire team got demotivated. Then our commission checks started coming late, or not showing up at all. Morale kept plunging over the next few months, as reps were owed tens or even hundreds of thousands of dollars in missing commissions.

Just as they had at Platinum, our best salespeople—the carnivores—were the first to jump ship. This prompted me to move myself and my whole team over to Solcius, a new solar company, where I opened up their new direct sales division as VP of sales. But the herbivores were stuck with far fewer options, often just hanging on and hoping things would improve.

A few years after that, I took the opportunity to start my own sales and leadership training company, the D2D Experts.

All these experiences taught me that even a seemingly wonderful company can get into trouble and lose its mojo, its integrity, or both. Ultimately, you can't count on any company to take care of you. You can only count on the value of your own skills and drive, which no company or boss can ever take away from you.

76

Sales Mastery

WHAT DOES IT FEEL LIKE when you actually achieve mastery at sales? It's a different moment of recognition for everyone. My moment happened to come on a Utah mountain, on a bright and beautiful winter morning.

My company was planning a high-end mastermind event for CEOs, where a small, highly selective group would get advanced coaching plus networking with their peers. The package cost $35,000. I had a phone appointment for 10:00 a.m. with a CEO who was thinking about signing up for the mastermind, but wasn't sure yet if it was worth that steep price.

The night before, however, new snow had coated my favorite local mountain with perfect powder for snowboarding. For a snowboarding nut like me, this meant that I *had to* get on the mountain immediately. I decided to bring my phone and AirPods and do the call from the slopes. I called the CEO at ten while riding up the chairlift, and we talked for about fifteen minutes. He had no idea I was outside, so we were all good.

But I just couldn't wait to finish the call before starting my first snowboarding run. I hit the slopes while still pitching this CEO, navigating my way between the trees and the other snowboarders on my backcountry trail. When I was about halfway down this huge mountain, he said, "What are you doing? I hear you breathing hard and air whooshing."

I replied, "Well, I have to be honest with you. I'm doing a snowboarding run right now. It's a beautiful day and the powder is perfect. And now I'm going to do a three sixty." I stopped talking long enough to lift off and do a 360-degree spin.

Somewhere in the back of my mind, I knew I was risking my sale. This guy might think I was being massively disrespectful and hang up on me. But my gut told me this was the right thing to do. It wasn't a plan, just a hunch that my authenticity would impress him.

The CEO replied, "Are you f——g kidding me?! You're doing this sale while flying down a mountain?!" He paused for a few seconds, then continued. "You know what? I'm in for thirty-five grand. Anyone crazy enough to do a sales pitch on a snowboard must have something to teach me." I later found out that he was also really into outdoor adventure and made a point of blocking time for his hobbies. He did our mastermind and loved it.

The point of this story isn't that you should do a pitch from a snowboard. It's probably safer for both your health and your closing rate if you don't!

The point, rather, is that after years of practicing and studying and trial and error, your instincts will kick in and take you to unconventional places. You are not a robot or an AI algorithm that spits out logical answers to every prompt. You're a quirky, unique human, and you can use your humanity to build rapport with customers. Not with all of them, but with enough of them in enough situations.

At some point you will internalize all the skills and insights you've learned, and you can just trust the Force.

That's sales mastery. And that can be your future.

•

77

Your Life Is More Than Your Career

THIS WHOLE BOOK has been about working and grinding and making money through the magic of sales. I'm still passionate about all of that and always will be. I want to grab strangers on the street and shake them, to explain how much money they could be making and how much better their quality of life could be if they embraced the life of a sales carnivore.

But as this book winds down, I also want to leave you with another message: your life is more than your career. As much as I want you to study and practice sales, to constantly improve your skills, I also want you to find harmony and balance. The old saying is true: working to live is better than living to work.

I meet many salespeople who get so obsessed with grinding that they stop having a life. They're not socializing or taking vacations or even chilling on the weekend. I feel bad for them, because they've lost their way. The goal of a sales carnivore is not just making money but having a life—an *epic* life!

As you think about your financial goals, it's great to save up for a house, a retirement account, your kids' education, and some investment-grade real estate. By all means, hire a qualified financial adviser and do all those sober, adult things that people with money do to sustain and grow their net worth.

But at the same time, don't forget to have fun! Once you can afford it, give yourself permission to splurge on a nice car, an exotic vacation, maybe even Super Bowl tickets. Use your success to enjoy the experiences you've always dreamed about. Every time I do something like that, I never regret it.

Finding this kind of harmony requires allocating your time just as strategically as you allocate your money. Remember near the beginning of the book, when we talked about your sales goals? One of the key variables was how many weeks a year you wanted to work. Think hard about that number! So many Americans barely take one week of vacation a year. Why not set up your life so you can take four weeks off with your loved ones? Or six? Or even eight?

You may think you get all the satisfaction you need from watching your bank account and investments grow. But those numbers are ultimately just a means to an end. Your actual goal should be nurturing your personal relationships and creating awesome experiences and moments of joy.

The ultimate state of harmony is when you truly enjoy both your work and your life. If you keep practicing what you've learned in this book, doing sales will feel more and more like fun rather than a grind. You may even get to the point that you don't *need* vacations to recharge your batteries, but you still *want* them for amazing experiences with your loved ones.

I know this idealistic vision might feel very far away at this point in your journey. For now at least, sales may still feel like a huge grind. You keep knocking doors or cold-calling, and you face a ton of rejection. A lot of prospects are total jerks, which hurts even though you know you shouldn't let it hurt. And even when you have a good day, you're still getting your face kicked in for at least half the day. I totally get it. I've been there too!

But you have to believe that it can get a lot better. And it *will* get better, if you keep at it and maintain a healthy and strong mindset. You can find joy in the little moments of each workday, even the hard days.

Remember the last time you had a fun conversation with some nice woman who talked your ear off? Even if she didn't buy from you, that time wasn't wasted. You practiced your craft. You made a new friend. You got to smile on a random Tuesday afternoon. How many people in this country work their butts off every day without any of those benefits?

Don't think of winning and fun as opposites—they're completely tied together. The more deals you close, the more fun you'll have while selling. The more fun you're having, the more positive energy you'll project. The more positive energy, the more deals you'll close. It's a virtuous circle that can carry you to the life of your dreams—if only you can get that circle cranking.

Meanwhile, of course, you also need to avoid spiraling downward into the opposite kind of vicious circle: fewer sales → no fun → depression → bad attitude → fewer sales.

Above all, don't beat yourself up about where you are on your unique sales journey, especially compared with anyone else. You're here right now, and where you are right now is just fine.

YOUR LIFE IS MORE THAN YOUR CAREER

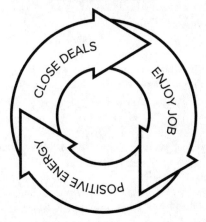

You can learn from your past without obsessing over it.

You can plan for your future without daydreaming about "some-day . . ."

You can find peace and contentment in the moment, whatever that looks like.

So if you asked me to sum up the big picture in a few bullets that you can tape to your bathroom mirror:

- Commit to being the best sales carnivore you can be.
- Keep improving and practicing your skills.
- Enjoy the process of selling, not just the results.
- Enjoy downtime and vacations with your loved ones.
- Beat your financial goals, then set new, bigger goals.
- Save for your future and invest wisely.
- Give back to charity.
- Take care of your body, mind, and soul.
- Remember that everything is part of the game.
- Play with no regrets.

I wish you the very best on your journey.

Acknowledgments

MY SINCERE THANKS to everyone who made this book possible, one way or another:

Everyone at my company, the D2D Experts. You guys rock.

Everyone at my publisher, Portfolio/Penguin, especially Megan Wenerstrom and Helen Healey-Cunningham.

My literary agent, Anthony Mattero.

My writing collaborator, Will Weisser.

Some of the sales icons who have inspired me: Myron Golden, Brian Tracy, Zig Ziglar, and Jordan Belfort.

Some of my earliest trainers in the sales world: Nick Hansen, Rico Rivera, Jeff Mendez, Casey Baugh, and Bryan Jackson.

All the experts who have spoken at our conferences and other events.

My parents, Jane and Paul.

My siblings, Spencer, Kelli, Abi, Emily, and Sophie.

My amazing daughters, Ellie, Nora, and Rosie.

My stepson Alton, who might be the most naturally gifted salesman I've ever met.

And last but definitely not least, my loving wife DeAnna, who supports me through all the crazy ups and downs of my entrepreneurial life. So happy to be sharing this journey with you!

More Resources from the D2D Experts

Here's a link that will take you to lots of useful resources offered by The D2D Experts:

thesamtaggart.com/eatwhatyoukill

Among the powerful things you'll find there:

My Previous Books

The ABC's of Closing—an expanded version of the closing part of the book you've just read.

The Self Xperience—my manifesto about personal empowerment and going after the life you really want, not the one you think you're supposed to want.

Our Apps and Software

Xpand—our human development system for coaches, managers, and sales reps. This app will help you level up your goal tracking, assignment management, routines, billing, rewards, and more. It's eight powerful software tools merged into a single app (xpandapp.io).

D2DCRM—our free, customizable CRM app, designed for the unique needs of D2D reps and their teams. It will simplify your workflow and make it easier to manage your prospects and customers, from initial list-building research through closing and post-closing follow-ups (thed2dcrm.com).

Vanilla Message, our unique app for texting prospects more effectively and with less time and effort. It will help you increase customer engagement via messaging campaigns, which will pay off via more deals, more positive reviews, more customer retention, and a more visible online presence (vanillamessage.com).

Our Training Video Courses

D2D University—our online education platform, featuring dozens of courses and hundreds of training videos for reps who want to improve their skills. Courses range from general sales training to the nitty-gritty details of specialized fields such as solar, roofing, and pest control (thed2dexperts.com/services/door-to-door-university).

Our Conferences and Events

D2DCON—our flagship annual conference, the largest in the world focused on D2D sales. Held every January, D2DCON attracts thousands of attendees, dozens of vendors, lots of breakout workshops, fun networking events, and more than fifty speakers who are A-list experts in their fields. Previous speakers have included Jordan Peterson, Ed Mylett, John Maxwell, Tim Grover, and Eric Thomas. This has become a can't-miss annual gathering for anyone serious about D2D sales (d2dcon.com).

Sales Bootcamp—our intense, two-day, in-person sales training event (thed2dexperts.com/services/sales-bootcamp).

Business Bootcamp—our two-day in-person business and leadership development event (thed2dexperts.com/services/door-to-door -boot-camp).

Our Sales Coaching and Consulting Services

We offer personalized sales coaching and consulting, either one-on-one or for teams, in person or virtually (thed2dexperts.com/services /door-to-door-consulting).

The *D2D Podcast*

Sales tips, tricks, and strategies for door-to-door salespeople. Featuring my cool interviews with a range of experts (podcasts.apple.com/us/podcast/the-d2d-podcast/id1231680638).

My Private Speaking Engagements

I'm available to speak to your organization about sales and leadership (thesamtaggart.com).

And More . . .

Please explore our website for even more content: thed2dexperts.com.

Please email us with any questions: info@thed2dexperts.com.

My Favorite Books (Other Than Mine)

HERE ARE SOME OF the most useful books I've ever read, other than the ones I wrote myself. Some are directly about sales; others are about mindset, habits, and other important subjects. Here they are in alphabetical order:

Awareness by Anthony De Mello
Atomic Habits by James Clear
Bulls, Owls, Lambs and Tigers by Charles J. Clarke III
The Closer's Survival Guide by Grant Cardone
The Compound Effect by Darren Hardy
Elastic Habits by Stephen Guise
The Miracle Morning by Hal Elrod
Never Split the Difference by Chris Voss
The Platinum Rule by Tony Alessandra and Michael O'Connor
The Psychology of Selling by Brian Tracy
SPIN Selling by Neil Rackham